LEAN AND Lavish

Weight Watchers®

*Fabulous recipes
to help
you keep
in shape
by Ann Page-Wood*

NEW ENGLISH LIBRARY

For information about the Weight Watchers classes, contact:
Weight Watchers UK Limited
11 Fairacres
Dedworth Road
Windsor
Berkshire SL4 4UY
Telephone: (0753) 856751

Art Director: Roger Judd
Editor: Heather Shackleton
Photography: Simon Smith at Barry Bullough's Studios
assisted by Glen Perotte
Line Drawings: Wendy Brammell
Food prepared by Ann Page-Wood
Stylist: Kathy Man

British Library Cataloguing in Publication Data

Page-Wood, Ann
   Lean and lavish.
   1. Food: Low calorie dishes – Recipes
   I. Title   II. Weight Watchers
   641.5'635

   ISBN 0-450-48502-1

First published in Great Britain in 1988 by New English Library, Mill Road, Dunton Green,
Sevenoaks, Kent, a division of Hodder & Stoughton Limited.

Photoset by Rowland Phototypesetting Limited,
Bury St Edmunds, Suffolk

Printed and bound by Hazell, Watson and Viney Limited,
Member of BPCC, Aylesbury, Bucks

CONTENTS

GENERAL INTRODUCTION

If you enjoy delicious food and are interested in losing weight healthily, *Lean and Lavish* is the book for you.

We're always being told what we should and shouldn't eat. It's confusing at the best of times, but help is at hand! The Weight Watchers Quick Start Plus Programme, on which this book is based, was devised by a team of eminent nutritionists to help remove some of the mystery surrounding healthy eating, and the Programme is constantly being revised to keep up to date with current research and trends.

Packed full of sumptuous recipes and mouthwatering colour photographs, *Lean and Lavish* will help you to become slim and healthy – and stay that way – by encouraging you to choose, prepare and cook the highest quality ingredients in the best ways possible.

Fish

Always buy fish when it's really fresh – shiny, bright-eyed and unblemished – store it in the refrigerator and use as soon as possible. White fish contains very little fat compared with the oilier varieties such as herrings, mackerel and sardines. However, all varieties are extremely nutritious. Smoked fish has a high salt content so there's no need to add extra salt when you're cooking it. Shellfish are usually sold ready-cooked and only need reheating (see Curried Prawns, page 62). Always drain the brine or oil from canned fish before using in a recipe, and when you buy frozen fish, take it home, preferably in an insulated bag, and transfer straight to the freezer.

Meat and Poultry

Buy meat which is as lean as possible, and remove any visible fat before cooking. Unless red meats like beef, lamb, pork or ham are to be marinated, as in Peppercorn Pork (page 206), place it on a rack and bake or grill until the fat stops dripping before using in a recipe. Mince should be formed into patties before grilling. Alternatively, boil the meat in water for a few minutes, allow to cool quickly and remove the fat which will solidify on the surface.

A high proportion of poultry fat is stored under the skin, so remove the skin before or after cooking.

Dairy Products

Milk, cheese and eggs provide a useful source of protein, minerals and other nutrients. We use only skimmed milk in our recipes, but we've included small quantities of single and soured cream to add a touch of luxury to certain dishes. Low-fat yogurt and fromage frais make a very good alternative to cream and we've used them in a number of recipes ranging from sweet and savoury dishes to salad dressings and drinks. To avoid curdling, hot dishes, like Beef Goulash (page 33), should be removed from the heat before the yogurt is added.

7

Top: Cherry Choux Puffs *(p. 214) Centre:* Beef Marsala *(p 208) Bottom:* Star Starter *(p 192)*

Here is a recipe for low-fat natural yogurt which is extremely simple and very economical to make. Your first batch will have to be made using a commercial yogurt as the 'starter', but you can use your own yogurt as the starter for future batches. Eventually, though, you'll have to start again with a commercial brand. Always make sure that your equipment is spotlessly clean.

2½oz (75g) powdered skimmed milk
water
1½ teaspoons low-fat natural yogurt
5fl oz (150ml) = 1 Milk Exchange

Total Calories: 250

1. Place the powdered milk in a measuring jug, gradually add the water to make 1 pint (600ml) of milk.
2. Pour the milk into a saucepan and bring to the boil, stirring occasionally to prevent whey. Simmer for 1 minute.
3. Leave the milk to cool to 42°C, 106°F.
4. Measure the commercial yogurt into a bowl, whisk in 2 tablespoons of the warm milk. Gradually add the remaining milk. Transfer to a warmed, wide-necked vacuum flask and leave undisturbed for 6–7 hours.
5. Pour off the whey and transfer the yogurt to a chilled basin. Whisk to enable the yogurt to cool quickly.
6. Cover the basin and refrigerate for at least 4 hours, which allows the yogurt to thicken.

Ideal for all sorts of savoury and sweet dishes, fromage frais and low-fat cheeses – cottage, curd and cheese spreads up to 50 Calories an ounce – are widely used throughout the book. We've kept cheeses with a higher fat content to the minimum, but they can be used in moderation – a little freshly grated Parmesan may make all the difference to a sauce or salad.

Eggs, eaten on their own or used in recipes, are extremely versatile, but we recommend that you restrict yourself to seven per week as they have a high fat content.

Fats

Our recipes include oils, polyunsaturated margarine, low-fat spread, mayonnaise and low-calorie salad dressings in restricted quantities. All polyunsaturated margarines tend to be soft, so store small quantities in the freezer for when you want to use the rubbing in method for crumble toppings and shortcrust pastry, etc.

Fruit and Vegetables

Good quality fruit and vegetables are available throughout the year, and to enjoy them at their best, either eat them raw or cook them for a very short time in a small amount of water – you may even be able to use the cooking liquid in a sauce or gravy if it's suitable. Avoid peeling fruit and vegetables unless it's absolutely necessary – just make sure they're well washed – and if you need to peel or slice them, do this immediately before they're cooked.

Herbs and Spices

Valued for many thousands of years, herbs and spices are currently enjoying a revival of interest, and lots of people are now growing their own in gardens, window boxes and flower pots. Although most of the recipes in this book refer to dried herbs, it's always better to use fresh if you can – just treble the amount, e.g. 1 teaspoon of dried rosemary equals 1 tablespoon of fresh, chopped rosemary.

To store fresh herbs, place them in a jar of water in the refrigerator, covered loosely with a plastic bag, and change the water daily. Parsley will stay fresh for 1–2 weeks kept this way.

Dried herbs keep even longer and if you wish to dry your own, tie them in bunches, hang in a cool, dark, airy space, then strip the leaves from the stems and store in dark jars away from direct light. Alternatively, dry the herbs in a microwave oven according to the manufacturer's instructions.

Spices should also be kept in dark, airtight containers away from the light. Whole spices, which you grind or grate yourself when required, will stay pungent far longer than ground spices, which tend to lose their flavour fairly quickly.

Here is a list of some of the numerous herbs and spices available.

Herb or Spice	Description
Allspice	The mild, spicy taste resembles cloves and cinnamon. Use as whole berries, crush and add to marinades or grind and include in a wide variety of sweet recipes.
Basil	In my opinion this is a herb to be treasured with its strong, sweet, pungent flavour. Use in savoury dishes, particularly with tomatoes and pasta.
Bay	The sweet bay tree leaves have a strong, spicy flavour. Use sparingly in stocks and casseroles. Bay, together with thyme, marjoram and parsley, make up the well-known bouquet garni.
Caper	Capers have a strong, aromatic flavour and are sold in their pickling liquid as they must not dry out. The caper is the unopened flower of the caper bush. Use in sauces and relishes and with fish and chicken recipes.
Caraway	The caraway seed has a spicy, rather sharp flavour. Add to vegetables such as cabbage, meat recipes and sweet dishes. The seeds may be chewed after a meal to sweeten the breath.
Cardamom	Whole cardamom pods contain tiny seeds which have a strong, spicy taste. Remove the seeds and either leave whole or crush before adding to recipes. Use to flavour sweet and savoury dishes. Ground cardamom can be bought but it loses its flavour quickly.
Chives	Chives have a mild onion flavour. The mauve flowers may also be used with the chopped chives in salads. Use in a wide variety of savoury dishes or as a garnish.
Cinnamon	Cinnamon is the dried inner bark of the cinnamon tree. It has a slightly sweet, fragrant, spicy taste and may be used in sticks to flavour drinks or syrups, or ground and incorporated in a wide range of sweet recipes.
Cloves	Cloves have a strong, pungent flavour. They may be used whole or ground in marinades and savoury and sweet dishes.

Coriander   Coriander leaves are used in savoury recipes and as a garnish. The seeds have an aromatic flavour and may be used whole or crushed and added to curries and sweet dishes.

Cumin   Cumin is a strong-smelling spice which can be used as a whole seed or crushed. It is an important ingredient of curries and widely used in savoury recipes.

Dill   Dill leaves have a delicate flavour, but the seeds are much more pungent. The leaves are used in salads or savoury recipes, particularly fish, and the seeds are often added to pickles and vinegar.

Elder   Elderflowers are slightly spicy and bitter and are used to flavour fruit recipes. Elderberries should never be eaten raw, but may be used to flavour pies, wines and syrups.

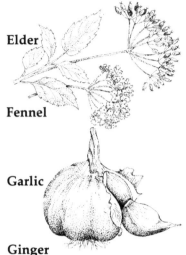

Fennel   Fennel is related to dill but has a stronger, slightly anise flavour. The fennel grown to use as a herb differs from the vegetable fennel plant. It is used in the same way as dill, but fennel seed is sometimes added to apple pies and chewed to sweeten the breath.

Garlic   Garlic has a strong, pungent flavour which lingers on the breath. The whole clove can be used unpeeled in stews, then discarded before serving. More often the clove is peeled, crushed or chopped and added to savoury recipes.

Ginger   Ginger is highly aromatic and spicy, with a slight lemon scent and a hot flavour. It is available as a whole fresh or dried root, ground or preserved. Use in curries, soups and sweet recipes.

Horseradish   Raw horseradish is very hot and pungent. It is traditionally served as a sauce accompaniment to beef but may be used in many savoury dishes.

Lovage   Lovage has a slightly spicy taste and may be added to vegetables while they're cooking or to a variety of savoury recipes.

Mace and Nutmeg   The fruit of the nutmeg tree, when ripe, splits to reveal a kernel, which contains the brown nutmeg wrapped in a bright red covering, mace. Both are dried and the mace turns a yellow-brown colour. Both are sold whole or ground and are used in sweet and savoury dishes. It is better to keep whole nutmeg and grate it just before use.

Marjoram and Oregano   There are different varieties of marjoram – wild marjoram is the same as oregano. Both have a sweet, spicy flavour. Use in savoury dishes, particularly tomato and pasta recipes.

Mint   There are many different varieties of mint. All have a distinctive and refreshing smell but vary slightly according to the species – eau de cologne, apple, peppermint, spearmint, etc. Use in sweet or savoury recipes.

Mustard   White mustard seeds have a slightly nutty flavour, while black are more pungent. Whole, powdered or prepared mustards are used in a wide variety of dishes. White mustard seedlings are sold with cress as a salad ingredient.

Parsley

Parsley has a tangy, slightly sweet flavour. The two main varieties differ in that one has a curly leaf and the other a flat leaf. Use raw in salads, as a garnish or in cooked savoury recipes.

Pepper

There are many varieties of pepper available. Green peppercorns, which are unripened white and black peppercorns, are sold in brine and should be rinsed before use. Black peppercorns are sun-dried green peppercorn berries sold whole or ground and used throughout this book. White peppercorns are ripe berries which are not as strong as the black corns. They are also available whole or ground. Other peppers include cayenne, which is ground from a red chilli pepper and very hot, and paprika, which varies from hot to mild.

Rosemary

Rosemary has a strong, aromatic scent with a pungent flavour. It is usually used in savoury dishes but may be added in small quantities to fruit recipes.

Saffron

Saffron has an aromatic, spicy and slightly bitter flavour and imparts a bright yellow colour to food. It can be bought whole or as a powder. Use with rice or in traditional Spanish dishes.

Sage

Sage has a pungent, slightly bitter flavour with a hint of camphor. Use in salads or cooked savoury dishes.

Tarragon

There are different varieties of tarragon. French tarragon is said to have the best flavour – sweet but also slightly bitter. It is used in salads, to flavour vinegar and in many cooked savoury recipes.

Thyme

There are over one hundred varieties of thyme but all have a strong, slightly sharp flavour. Use sparingly or it will overpower other flavours. It is an ingredient of the traditional bouquet garni. Although thyme is mainly used in savoury dishes, lemon thyme adds an interesting flavour to fruit salads.

Turmeric

Turmeric has a delicate, slightly peppery flavour and gives a yellow colour to food. It is an essential ingredient in curry powders and widely used in savoury dishes.

Vanilla

The vanilla pod is the fruit of the vanilla orchid vine. It is sold when dried and has a sweet, delicate flavour. It is also available as a liquid extract. Use in milk dishes, cakes and breads.

HEALTHY COOKING TECHNIQUES

How is it possible to cook food in ways which are healthy and help retain its natural flavour and goodness? Start with high-quality, nutritious ingredients, use the methods outlined below and your meals will not only taste good, they'll be lower in calories, too.

Grilling and Barbecuing

Grills have been commonplace in most kitchens for decades, but barbecuing has only recently gained its huge popularity. Both methods rely on the food being held under or over radiant heat – excellent for slimmers because any fat simply melts and drips away. Try grilling or barbecuing tender, even-sized cuts of meat, or oily fish like mackerel, herrings and sardines. Firm-fleshed white fish can also be cooked this way, but brush frequently with oil or a marinade to keep it moist. Tomatoes, mushrooms and peppers can be cooked on their own or skewered together, with or without cubes of meat or fish, to create delicious kebabs.

Oven Cooking

Baking, roasting, casseroling and braising are all carried out in the oven. Baking and roasting are both methods which are suitable for good quality cuts of meat. Place the meat on a rack over the roasting pan and allow the fat to drip away.

To bake 'en papillote', first wrap your fish, meat or poultry in foil or non-stick baking parchment. It will cook in its own juices and stay succulent and full of flavour. Oven bricks work on the same principle, but as with en papillote, meat will not take on the brown colour of a traditional roasted joint.

Slow-Cooking

Slow cookers are a boon for the cook with little time to spare. Simply prepare your meal in the morning and leave it to cook slowly during the day. Served with lightly cooked vegetables, you'll be sure of a delicious, warming meal at the end of your busy day.

Microwaving

The microwave oven has revolutionised modern cooking. Particularly useful for defrosting and reheating frozen foods, and economically cooking single portions, it's a method which is fast, efficient and nutritionally sound. All the microwave recipes included in this book have been tested in a 650 watt oven.

Stir-Frying

An excellent way of retaining the natural goodness of food, stir-frying is widely used throughout the book. The ideal pan to use is a wok, and these are available in many forms – round-bottomed for gas, flat-bottomed for electric hobs, traditional carbon steel and free-standing electric – but if you don't have a wok, use a saucepan or a deep-sided frying pan. You only need a small amount of fat and, as the name implies, the ingredients, which should be small and evenly sized, are constantly stirred to keep them in contact with the hot sides of the pan.

To help prevent food from sticking to them, woks and frying pans need 'proving' or 'seasoning'. Clean the pan well, sprinkle with salt, place over a low heat, tip the salt out and wipe the inside with kitchen paper until the paper wipes clean. Then heat a little oil in the pan and wipe it again with kitchen paper. Carbon steel pans should be washed, dried and then wiped with a little oil to prevent them from rusting.

Steaming

Cooked without fat or water, steamed food retains a high percentage of goodness and is nutritionally excellent. Steamers come in many shapes and sizes – a saucepan base with a top compartment, a simple Japanese basket, Chinese bamboo, those which fit on top of woks and sophisticated electric steamers – but they all perform the same function. If you don't have a steamer, fit a metal colander or sieve over a pan of simmering water and cover with a saucepan lid.

FAMILY FAVOURITES

Healthy eating is a way of life, not just a fad for the weight conscious. It is vitally important to educate children to recognise which foods should be included in their diet and to discourage them from eating highly refined processed foods which tend to be high in fat, sugar and salt.

It isn't always easy to persuade children to eat wholemeal bread, rice or pasta, but try gradually introducing these foods in different forms. Use wholemeal breadcrumbs in stuffings or as a coating for fishcakes, etc., add wholemeal pasta to soups like Minestrone (page 18) and serve main course dishes like Frankfurter Bake (page 40) with baked jacket potatoes and fresh green vegetables.

Some ever-popular sweet desserts are included in this section, but gradually decrease the amount of sugar you use when cooking fruit, and use less refined flour to make crumble toppings.

Children and teenagers have higher energy requirements than adults, so compensate for this by serving them with larger portions of lightly cooked vegetables and fruit. Try to encourage them away from unhealthy 'junk' food and provide nutritious alternatives.

With the busy working mum in mind, we've included some recipes which make use of a slow cooker, but details of the conventional cooking methods are also given.

The majority of recipes in this section can be successfully frozen and reheated, so if you live alone or only cook for one or two people, you can still enjoy these delicious, wholesome recipes.

SMOKED FISH CHOWDER

Serves 4

180 Calories per serving

This makes a particularly delicious lunch and can be taken to work or to school in vacuum flasks to keep it hot.

1 teaspoon margarine

1 onion, chopped

4½oz (135g) potato, chopped into small cubes

1 pint (600ml) skimmed milk

13oz (390g) smoked cod or haddock fillet

bay leaf

salt and pepper

lemon juice

2 tablespoons chopped parsley

Exchanges per serving: Bread ¼
Fat ¼
Milk ½
Protein 2½
Vegetable ¼
15 Optional Calories

1. Melt the margarine in a saucepan, add the onion and stir-fry for 3 minutes.
2. Stir the potato and milk into the saucepan, lay the smoked fish fillets in the mixture, add a bay leaf; cover and simmer for about 15 minutes or until the potato is cooked. Remove and discard the bay leaf.
3. Using a fish slice, lift out the smoked cod or haddock and lay it on a plate. Remove the skin and separate the fish into large flakes.
4. Pour the milk, etc. into a blender or food processor, add about half the fish and process until smooth.
5. Return the puréed mixture to the saucepan and season to taste with salt, pepper and lemon juice. Stir in the reserved fish and parsley and bring to the boil, stirring all the time. Serve in warm soup bowls.

SPINACH SOUP

Serves 4

80 Calories per serving

Always wash fresh spinach several times in cold water to remove the dirt and grit which clings to the leaves. A sprinkling of freshly grated Parmesan cheese on the soup makes it extra good.

8oz (240g) spinach

3oz (90g) potato, diced

1 small onion, chopped

¾ pint (450ml) vegetable or chicken stock

3 tablespoons single cream

freshly grated nutmeg

salt and pepper

4 teaspoons grated Parmesan cheese

Exchanges per serving: Bread ¼
Vegetable 1
35 Optional
Calories

1. Wash the spinach and roughly chop the leaves and stalks.
2. Place the spinach, potato and onion in a saucepan. Pour in the stock. Bring to the boil, reduce the heat; cover and simmer for 20 minutes.
3. Transfer the spinach, stock, etc. to a blender or food processor and process until smooth.
4. Pour the spinach purée back into the saucepan and reheat, then stir in the cream and season with the nutmeg, salt and pepper.
5. Pour the soup into four warm soup bowls and sprinkle with the Parmesan cheese.

PUMPKIN SOUP

Serves 4

60 Calories per serving

This is a good way to use up the pumpkin flesh which is scooped out of a whole pumpkin for Halloween. If you buy the pumpkin as a wedge it should weigh about a pound (480g) or more as the skin and pips, which have to be discarded, are quite heavy.

2 teaspoons margarine

1 onion, chopped

12oz (360g) pumpkin flesh, cubed

3oz (90g) potato, chopped

1 stick of celery, chopped

1 pint (600ml) vegetable stock

2 teaspoons lemon juice

salt and pepper

Exchanges per serving: Bread ¼
Fat ½
Vegetable 1¼

1. Melt the margarine in a saucepan, add the onion and stir-fry for 3–4 minutes.
2. Stir in the pumpkin, potato, celery and stock. Bring to the boil, reduce the heat; cover and simmer for 30–35 minutes.
3. Transfer the pumpkin, stock, etc. to a blender or food processor and process until smooth.
4. Pour the pumpkin purée back into the saucepan, stir in the lemon juice and season to taste with salt and pepper. Stir the soup over a moderate heat, pour into warm soup bowls and serve immediately.

MINESTRONE

Serves 4

150 Calories per serving

This soup is wonderfully filling and should be served with a lunch or supper dish and accompanied by fresh fruit.

4 tomatoes, peeled and chopped

2 leeks, sliced

2 sticks celery, chopped

6oz (180g) carrots, diced

4oz (120g) small courgettes, sliced or chopped

4oz (120g) French beans, cut in 1-inch (2.5-cm) lengths

1½ teaspoons chopped basil

2 tablespoons chopped parsley

1¼ pints (750ml) vegetable stock

3oz (90g) drained canned haricot or kidney beans

2oz (60g) small pasta shells or other small pasta shapes

1oz (30g) Parmesan cheese, finely grated

Exchanges per serving: Bread ¾
Protein ¼
Vegetable 3

1. Place the tomatoes, leeks, celery, carrots, courgettes, French beans, herbs and stock in a saucepan. Bring to the boil over a moderate heat, cover, reduce the heat and simmer for 25 minutes.
2. Stir the canned beans and pasta into the saucepan; cover and simmer for a further 10 minutes.
3. Ladle the soup into four large warm bowls and sprinkle the cheese over each serving.

Creamy Cod and Prawns *(p 20)*

CREAMY COD AND PRAWNS

Serves 4

335 Calories per serving

The cod and prawn sauce is served in the middle of a potato and spinach border – an attractive as well as a delicious way of serving fish.

For the sauce:

12oz (360g) skinned cod fillet

3oz (90g) peeled prawns

9fl oz (270ml) skimmed milk

2 tablespoons chopped chives

1 tablespoon chopped parsley

salt and pepper

4 teaspoons margarine

8 teaspoons flour

1oz (30g) mature Cheddar cheese, grated

For the border:

1lb 2oz (540g) potatoes, cubed

salt

2 tablespoons skimmed milk

6oz (180g) spinach

good pinch of freshly grated nutmeg

1 tomato, sliced or cut in wedges to garnish

> **Exchanges per serving: Bread 1½**
> **Fat 1**
> **Milk ¼**
> **Protein 3½**
> **Vegetable ½**
> **20 Optional**
> **Calories**

1. Place the cod fillet and prawns in a pan, pour over the 9fl oz (270ml) of skimmed milk and add the chives and parsley. Season with a sprinkling of salt and pepper.
2. Heat the milk and fish over a moderate heat and simmer gently for 10–12 minutes or until the fish is cooked. Flake the cod.
3. Melt the margarine in a separate saucepan, add the flour and stir over the heat for 1 minute.
4. Gradually blend the milk and fish into the margarine and flour and bring to the boil, stirring all the time. Reserve a little grated cheese and stir the remainder into the sauce. Put to one side.
5. Boil the potatoes in salted water until soft; drain and transfer to a blender or food processor, add the milk and process until smooth. While the potatoes are cooking, wash and roughly chop the spinach. Place the spinach in a separate saucepan; cover and boil for about 4 minutes without any additional water. Drain and press out any liquid.
6. Add the spinach to the potatoes in the blender or food processor, add the nutmeg and process until smooth. Season to taste.
7. Pipe the hot potato and spinach mixture round the edge of a large, shallow au gratin or flameproof dish.
8. Heat the fish sauce, stirring all the time. Pour the sauce into the middle of the potato mixture and sprinkle with the reserved cheese.
9. Grill under a moderate heat until bubbling. Arrange the tomato on the top and return to the hot grill for a minute to warm the tomato.

STUFFED COD CUTLETS

Serves 4

210 Calories per serving

Wrap the cod fillets in non-stick baking parchment before cooking – you'll need less fat and save on Calories.

4 × 5-oz (150-g) cod cutlets

For the stuffing:

2 teaspoons margarine

1 onion, chopped

2oz (60g) mushrooms, chopped

4 teaspoons chopped parsley

1oz (30g) fresh wholemeal or white breadcrumbs

1oz (30g) cheese, grated

1 egg, lightly beaten

salt and pepper

Exchanges per serving: Bread ¼
Fat ½
Protein 4
Vegetable ½

1. Remove the bones from each cutlet.
2. Melt the margarine over a moderate heat, add the onion and stir-fry for 3–4 minutes. Add the mushrooms and stir-fry for a further 2 minutes.
3. Mix the onion, mushrooms, parsley, breadcrumbs and cheese together. Stir in the beaten egg and season well with salt and pepper.
4. Lay a large piece of non-stick baking parchment on a baking tray. Arrange the cod cutlets on the parchment, pile the stuffing in the centre and on the top of each cutlet, then fold the parchment over to seal.
5. Bake at Gas Mark 4, 180°C, 350°F for 25–30 minutes.

SKATE AU GRATIN

Serves 4

155 Calories per serving

Skate is at its best from September to April, although it's available all year round. This recipe uses the 'wings', which are full of flavour.

1 onion, chopped

4 tomatoes, skinned and chopped

2oz (60g) mushrooms, chopped

4 tablespoons white wine

½–1 teaspoon chopped basil

1 tablespoon chopped parsley

4 × 5-oz (150-g) pieces of skate 'wing'

salt and pepper

½oz (15g) fresh breadcrumbs

Exchanges per serving: Protein 3
Vegetable 1½
30 Optional
Calories

1. Place the onion, tomatoes, mushrooms, wine and herbs in a saucepan and bring to the boil, stirring occasionally. Reduce the heat to low and add the skate to the saucepan. Cover and simmer for 15–20 minutes or until the skate is cooked.
2. Transfer the skate to a warm ovenproof dish, cover and place in a warm oven.
3. Increase the heat under the saucepan to high and boil rapidly until the sauce is reduced by half. Season with salt and pepper.
4. Spoon the sauce over the skate, sprinkle with the breadcrumbs and transfer to a hot grill to brown the breadcrumbs.

FISHERMAN'S PIE

Serves 4

260 Calories per serving

Monkfish, sometimes called angler fish, is a firm-fleshed white fish with a central bone. If you buy the fish from a fishmonger, ask his advice on the weight of the bone as it varies according to where the cut is taken from. Alternatively, ask him to bone it for you.

10oz (300g) monkfish, cut in chunks, or about 13oz (390g) on the bone

7fl oz (210ml) skimmed milk

12oz (360g) potatoes

salt

1 tablespoon margarine

6oz (180g) leek, thinly sliced

3oz (90g) mushrooms, sliced

2 tablespoons flour

1 tablespoon cream cheese

1 tablespoon lemon juice

1½oz (45g) cheese, grated

pepper

Exchanges per serving: Bread 1
Fat ¾
Protein 2½
Vegetable ¾
60 Optional Calories

1. Place the monkfish in the milk; cover and simmer gently for about 5 minutes. Drain and reserve the liquor. If using a whole piece of monkfish, flake in large pieces off the bone.
2. Boil the potatoes in boiling salted water for 15–20 minutes until cooked. Drain.
3. Melt the margarine in a saucepan, add the leek and stir-fry for 3–4 minutes. Add the mushrooms, sprinkle in the flour and stir for a minute over a low heat.
4. Reserve 3 tablespoons of the liquor, then gradually blend the cream cheese and the remainder of the liquor into the leeks. Bring to the boil, stirring all the time. Add the fish and lemon juice and transfer to an ovenproof dish.
5. Mash the potatoes with the reserved liquor and cheese; season with salt and pepper. Either pipe the potatoes on top of the monkfish or spread over the fish and roughen the surface with a fork.
6. Bake in a preheated oven, Gas Mark 5, 190°C, 375°F for 20–25 minutes. If desired, place under a grill until well browned.

FRUIT-STUFFED HERRINGS

Serves 4

325 Calories per serving

This is a very economical recipe. Herrings are one of the cheapest fishes available and most fishmongers will clean and bone them for you in a matter of minutes.

4 × 4-oz (120-g) whole herring fillets

salt and pepper

For the stuffing:

1 teaspoon vegetable oil

1 small onion, finely chopped

1 medium eating apple, peeled, cored and chopped

2oz (60g) fresh wholemeal breadcrumbs

1 tablespoon chopped parsley

finely grated zest and juice of ½ a medium orange

2 tablespoons water

Exchanges per serving: Bread ½
Fat ¼
Fruit ¼
Protein 3
Vegetable ¼
5 Optional
Calories

1. Lay the herring fillets skin side down, season with a little salt and pepper.
2. Heat the oil, add the onion and stir-fry for 3–4 minutes. Mix in the chopped apple and stir-fry for a further 2 minutes. Remove from the heat.
3. Stir the onion and apple into the bread-crumbs, mix in the parsley and orange zest and stir in the orange juice to bind the stuffing together.
4. Place a spoonful of the stuffing in the centre of each fillet, then roll the herring round it. Transfer to an ovenproof dish.
5. Spoon the water round the stuffed fillets, cover with foil and bake at Gas Mark 4, 180°C, 350°F for 25–30 minutes.

TUNA AND SWEETCORN FLAN

Serves 6
255 Calories per serving

This may be served hot or cold. It is an easy meal to wrap and take on a picnic or for a packed lunch.

For the flan case:

5oz (150g) wholemeal or plain flour

pinch of salt

4 tablespoons margarine

5–6 teaspoons ice-cold water

1 tablespoon wholemeal or plain flour for rolling out the pastry

For the filling:

1 teaspoon margarine

1 leek, thinly sliced

1 small green or red pepper, cored, seeded and chopped

3oz (90g) drained canned sweetcorn

6oz (180g) drained canned tuna, flaked

2 eggs

¼ pint (150ml) skimmed milk

1 tablespoon chopped parsley

salt and pepper

1 tomato, sliced

Exchanges per serving: Bread 1
Fat 2
Protein 1¼
Vegetable ½
25 Optional
Calories

1. First of all, make the pastry. Stir the flour and salt together in a bowl.
2. Add the margarine which, if possible, has been stored in the freezer. Rub it into the flour using the tips of your fingers and thumbs until the mixture resembles fresh breadcrumbs.
3. Using a round-bladed knife, mix the cold water into the pastry to form a dough. If time allows, wrap the pastry in foil or clingfilm and chill for 20–30 minutes.
4. Dust the rolling pin and a sheet of non-stick baking parchment with the remaining flour. Roll out the pastry a little larger than the 7½-inch (19-cm) flan ring. Carefully line the flan ring with the pastry, gently pressing it down the sides.
5. Trim the top edge. Lay a piece of baking parchment in the flan, weigh it down with a few dried beans or rice and bake at Gas Mark 6, 200°C, 400°F for 10 minutes, then remove the baking parchment and beans and bake for a further 4–5 minutes. Remove from the oven.
6. Prepare the filling. Melt the margarine in a pan, add the leek and chopped pepper and stir-fry for 4–5 minutes.
7. Mix the leek, pepper, sweetcorn and tuna together. Lightly beat the eggs and milk together, pour into the tuna mixture and add the parsley and a sprinkling of salt and pepper.
8. Spoon the filling into the baked flan case and return to a preheated oven, Gas Mark 4, 180°C, 350°F for 25–30 minutes.
9. If the flan is to be served hot, arrange the slices of tomato on top and return to the oven for about 3 minutes. If it is to be served cold, remove from the oven, cool and garnish with the tomato before serving.

CHICKEN IN A POT

Serves 4

275 Calories per serving

Compared to chicken breasts, boneless skinned chicken thighs are very economical and are now available in supermarkets.

12fl oz (360ml) chicken stock

1 tablespoon cornflour

1 large onion, chopped

5oz (150g) carrots, diced

5-oz (150-g) mixture of parsnip, swede and turnip, diced

1lb 4oz (600g) skinned and boned chicken thighs

1 tablespoon tomato purée

½ teaspoon tarragon

2oz (60g) mushrooms, sliced

4oz (120g) fast-boil long grain rice

salt and pepper

1 tablespoon chopped parsley

1. Blend a little of the stock into the cornflour and put to one side.
2. Pour the remaining stock into a saucepan, add the onion, carrots, parsnips, etc., chicken, tomato purée and tarragon. Bring to the boil over a moderate heat, stir in the cornflour paste and boil for 1–2 minutes, stirring all the time.
3. Reduce the heat, cover the saucepan and simmer for 30 minutes, stirring occasionally.
4. Stir in the mushrooms and rice and boil for 5–10 minutes until the rice is tender. Season well with salt and pepper and transfer to a warm serving dish. Sprinkle with parsley and serve.

Exchanges per serving: Bread 1
Protein 4
Vegetables 1½
10 Optional
Calories

TURKEY PIE

Serves 4

315 Calories per serving

If you've bought a large turkey for Christmas or Easter and are left with a lot of cooked meat, instead of serving it cold with salads, why not try this quick and simple pastry crust pie.

For the pastry:

3oz (90g) wholemeal or plain flour

pinch of salt

8 teaspoons margarine

approximately 1 tablespoon ice-cold water

1 tablespoon wholemeal or plain flour for rolling out the pastry

2 teaspoons skimmed milk

For the filling:

12oz (360g) cooked turkey

¼ pint (150ml) skimmed milk

4fl oz (120ml) chicken or vegetable stock

4 teaspoons cornflour

9oz (270g) cooked diced mixed vegetables such as carrots, peas, swede

2 tablespoons chopped spring onion

salt and pepper

Exchanges per serving: Bread ¾
Fat 2
Protein 3
Vegetable ¾
30 Optional
Calories

---

1. First of all, make the pastry. Stir the flour and salt together in a small bowl.
2. Add the margarine which, if possible, has been stored in the freezer. Rub it into the flour using the tips of your fingers and thumbs until the mixture resembles fresh breadcrumbs.
3. Using a round-bladed knife, mix the cold water into the pastry to form a dough. If time allows, wrap in clingfilm or foil and chill for 20–30 minutes.
4. Meanwhile, prepare the filling. Cut the turkey into cubes. Blend the milk and stock gradually into the cornflour and bring to the boil, stirring all the time. Reduce the heat and stir in the turkey, cooked vegetables and spring onion. Season to taste.
5. Transfer the turkey sauce to a 1½-pint (900-ml) pie dish and place a pie funnel in the centre to support the pastry crust.
6. Sprinkle the rolling pin and a sheet of non-stick baking parchment with the remaining flour and roll out the pastry a little larger than the pie dish.
7. Cut a strip from all the way round the pastry, moisten the rim of the pie dish with a little water and press the pastry strip onto it. Brush the pastry rim with a little water and cover with the pastry lid. Press the edges firmly together.
8. Trim the edge, press together once again and using the back of the knife 'knock' the two pieces of pastry together. If there are sufficient pastry trimmings, re-roll them and use to decorate the pastry lid.
9. Brush the pastry lid with the remaining milk and bake at Gas Mark 6, 200°C, 400°F for 15 minutes, then reduce the heat to Gas Mark 4, 180°C, 350°F for a further 25–30 minutes.

PORK IN CIDER

Serves 4

235 Calories per serving

I found that a loin chop weighing about 5½oz (165g) was only 4oz (120g) after the rind and visible fat had been removed before the initial grilling, so I suggest you look for lean chops weighing between 5oz and 5½oz (150g and 165g).

4 × 4-oz (120-g) pork loin chops

2 teaspoons vegetable oil

1 large onion, halved and sliced

1 green pepper, cored, seeded and sliced

2 sticks celery, chopped

½ pint (300ml) cider

5 teaspoons cornflour

2 tomatoes, peeled and chopped

8fl oz (240ml) chicken or vegetable stock

¾ teaspoon dried basil or 2–3 teaspoons fresh chopped basil

salt and pepper

**Exchanges per serving: Fat ½
Protein 2½
Vegetable 1¼
40 Optional
Calories**

1. Place the pork chops on a rack under a preheated grill and cook, turning once, until the fat has stopped dripping from the meat.
2. If the chops are to be cooked in the oven, heat the oil in an ovenproof casserole, but if you wish to use a slow-cooker, heat the oil in a flameproof casserole or saucepan. Add the onion and green pepper and stir-fry for 3 minutes.
3. Add the celery and stir-fry for a further 2–3 minutes.
4. Blend the cider and cornflour together and stir into the pan with the tomatoes, chops, stock and basil. Season with salt and pepper.
5. Bring to the boil over a moderate heat, stirring all the time.
6. Either cover the casserole and bake in a preheated oven, Gas Mark 4, 180°C, 350°F for 50–55 minutes, or transfer to a preheated slow-cooker, cover and switch to low for 6–7 hours.

PORK AND VEGETABLE BAKE

Serves 4

335 Calories per serving

This simple dish makes a thoroughly enjoyable warming meal. Serve with crisp hot vegetables such as calabrese broccoli or dwarf beans.

1lb 4oz (600g) minced pork

4fl oz (120ml) apple juice

¼ pint (150ml) vegetable stock

4 teaspoons cornflour

2 leeks, thinly sliced

6oz (180g) carrots, diced

½ teaspoon mixed herbs

For the topping:

9oz (270g) potatoes, diced

9oz (270g) swede, diced

salt

1 teaspoon margarine

1 tablespoon skimmed milk

pepper

1. Form the minced pork into small balls with dampened hands, place on a rack under a preheated grill and cook for 6–8 minutes, turning to brown all sides.
2. Blend the apple juice and stock with the cornflour, pour into a saucepan and add the leeks, carrots and herbs. Crumble in the pork and bring to the boil, stirring all the time. Cover and simmer for 10 minutes, stirring occasionally.
3. Boil the potatoes and swede in salted water for about 15 minutes or until tender. Drain.
4. Mash the potato and swede with the margarine and milk; season well with salt and pepper.
5. Transfer the pork mixture to a deep ovenproof dish. Spoon the swede and potato on top and spread to completely cover the pork. Roughen the surface with a fork.
6. Bake at Gas Mark 5, 190°C, 375°F for 30 minutes.

Exchanges per serving: Bread ¾
Fat ¼
Fruit ¼
Protein 4
Vegetable 2¼
10 Optional
Calories

POTATO AND HAM SALAD

Serves 4

200 Calories per serving

New potatoes, which are small and have a waxy texture, are the best type to use for potato salads but any variety may be used. Take care, though, not to overcook them or they will start to collapse.

9oz (270g) potatoes (preferably new)

salt

2 eggs

1 red pepper

4oz (120g) cooked ham, diced

3 tablespoons chopped spring onions

3oz (90g) drained canned sweetcorn

For the dressing:

2 tablespoons low-calorie mayonnaise

4 tablespoons low-fat natural yogurt

salt and pepper

lettuce, endive, chicory or Chinese cabbage leaves

1. Boil the potatoes in salted water for 15–20 minutes until just cooked. Drain.
2. Place the eggs in boiling water and simmer for 10 minutes. Drain, remove the shells and allow to cool.
3. Grill the red pepper under a moderate heat, turning frequently until black and blistering. Plunge in cold water and peel off the skin. Remove the core and seeds and chop the pepper.
4. Cut the potatoes into slices or cubes and chop the eggs.
5. Mix together the potatoes, eggs, chopped pepper, ham, spring onions and sweetcorn.
6. Stir the mayonnaise and yogurt together; season with salt and pepper. Spoon the dressing over the salad and carefully mix to cover all the ingredients.
7. Line a serving plate or bowl with the lettuce leaves, pile the salad in the centre and serve.

Exchanges per serving: Bread 1
Fat ¾
Protein 1½
Vegetable ½

BEEF CARBONNADE

Serves 4

370 Calories per serving

This traditional recipe has been adapted to suit the weight conscious. Use wholemeal, granary or white French bread, but dip it well into the gravy so it absorbs the flavour, then rises to the top and becomes crisp.

1lb 4oz (600g) stewing beef, e.g. chuck steak

2 teaspoons vegetable oil

1 clove garlic, chopped

2 onions, sliced

1 tablespoon flour

½ teaspoon mixed herbs

1 tablespoon vinegar

½ pint (300ml) brown ale

½ pint (300ml) beef stock

4 × ½-oz (15-g) slices French bread

approximately 2 teaspoons Dijon mustard

> **Exchanges per serving: Bread ½**
> **Fat ½**
> **Protein 4**
> **Vegetable ½**
> **35 Optional**
> **Calories**

1. Lay the beef on a rack under a hot grill and cook, turning once, for 6–8 minutes until brown. Allow to cool, then cut into 1½-inch (4-cm) cubes.
2. Heat the oil in an ovenproof casserole, add the garlic and onion and stir-fry for 3–4 minutes.
3. Add the flour to the casserole, stir over a moderate heat for a minute, then stir in the beef, herbs, vinegar, brown ale and stock. Bring to the boil, stirring all the time.
4. Cover the casserole and transfer to a preheated oven, Gas Mark 3, 160°C, 325°F for 2 hours.
5. Spread the four slices of French bread thickly with mustard and lay on top of the beef, pushing the bread into the gravy using the back of a tablespoon.
6. Return the carbonnade, uncovered, to the oven for a further 40 minutes until the bread is slightly crisp.

BEEF AND PUMPKIN CASSEROLE

Serves 4

335 Calories per serving

This makes a warming meal for a cold wintry night. To make it even more special, substitute some of the stock for red wine or beer and alter the Calories accordingly.

8 large dried prunes

1lb 2oz (540g) braising steak

1 tablespoon vegetable oil

1 large clove garlic, finely chopped

2 medium onions, chopped

1 green pepper, cored, seeded and sliced

4 teaspoons flour

2 tablespoons tomato purée

18fl oz (540ml) beef stock

6oz (180g) pumpkin, cubed

> **Exchanges per serving: Fat ¾**
> **Fruit 1**
> **Protein 3½**
> **Vegetable 1¼**
> **15 Optional**
> **Calories**

1. Cover the prunes with cold water and leave to soak for several hours or overnight. Drain and remove the stones.
2. Lay the steak on a rack under a hot grill and cook, turning once, for 6–8 minutes until brown. Allow to cool, then cut into 1½-inch (4-cm) cubes.
3. Heat the oil in an ovenproof casserole, add the garlic and onions and stir-fry for 3–4 minutes.
4. Add the green pepper and stir-fry for a further 2 minutes. Sprinkle in the flour and remove from the heat.
5. Gradually blend in the tomato purée and beef stock. Stir in the prunes, braising steak and pumpkin and bring to the boil over a moderate heat, stirring all the time.
6. Cover the casserole and transfer to the oven, Gas Mark 3, 160°C, 325°F for 1½ hours.

BEEF GOULASH

Serves 4

325 Calories per serving

*Take care to measure the paprika accurately. There are two varieties of paprika sold –
mild and hot – and this recipe uses the hot variety.*

1lb 4oz (600g) stewing beef, e.g. chuck steak

2 teaspoons vegetable oil

1 clove garlic, chopped

1 onion, roughly chopped

1 red pepper, cored, seeded and cut in strips

2 teaspoons hot paprika

4 teaspoons flour

14oz (397g) canned chopped tomatoes

¼ pint (150ml) beef stock

½ teaspoon chopped fresh basil or 2 teaspoons dried

1 bay leaf

4 tablespoons low-fat natural yogurt

**Exchanges per serving: Fat ½
Protein 4
Vegetable 2
15 Optional Calories**

1. Lay the beef on a rack under a hot grill and cook, turning once, for 6–8 minutes until brown. Allow to cool, then cut into 1½-inch (4-cm) cubes.
2. If the goulash is to be cooked in the oven, heat the oil in an ovenproof casserole, but if you wish to use a slow-cooker, heat the oil in a flameproof casserole or saucepan. Add the garlic and onion and stir-fry for 2–3 minutes.
3. Add the red pepper and stir-fry for a further 3 minutes.
4. Stir in the paprika and flour, mix well and add the beef, chopped tomatoes, stock, basil and bay leaf. Bring to the boil, stirring all the time.
5. Either cover the casserole and bake in a preheated oven, Gas Mark 3, 160°C, 325°F for 1¾–2 hours, or transfer to a preheated slow-cooker, cover and switch to low for 6–7 hours.
6. Remove and discard the bay leaf and serve each portion with a tablespoon of low-fat natural yogurt.

VEAL AND APRICOT CASSEROLE

Serves 4

265 Calories per serving

It's not necessary to precook veal in the same way as other red meats. The courgettes are added towards the end of the cooking time so they stay nice and crisp.

3oz (90g) dried apricots

14oz (420g) stewing veal

1 tablespoon vegetable oil

2 leeks, sliced

5 teaspoons flour

6oz (180g) drained canned sweetcorn

½ teaspoon marjoram

¾ pint (450ml) chicken or vegetable stock

salt and pepper

6oz (180g) courgettes, sliced

Exchanges per serving: Bread ½
Fat ¾
Fruit ¾
Protein 2½
Vegetable 1¼
15 Optional
Calories

1. Cover the apricots with cold water and leave overnight or for several hours. Drain.
2. Cut the veal into 1½-inch (4-cm) cubes.
3. Heat the oil in an ovenproof casserole or, if you wish to cook this recipe in a slow-cooker, use a saucepan. Add the leeks and stir-fry for 3–4 minutes.
4. Sprinkle the flour into the pan, stir it round and remove from the heat. Add the veal, apricots, sweetcorn and marjoram and gradually blend in the stock.
5. Bring to the boil over a moderate heat, stirring all the time, and season with salt and pepper. Cover and bake at Gas Mark 3, 160°C, 325°F for 1 hour 20 minutes. Stir in the courgettes, cover and return to the oven for a further 25 minutes. Alternatively, transfer to a preheated slow-cooker and cook on low for 5½ hours, then add the courgettes and continue cooking for a further 50 minutes.

Top: Fruit Condé *(p42)*
Bottom: Veal and Apricot Casserole

OATMEAL-COATED LIVER

Serves 4

405 Calories per serving

Remember the rubbery, flavourless liver of years ago? This method of cooking liver makes sure it stays tender and full of flavour.

15oz (450g) lamb's liver, sliced

2 tablespoons plain flour

salt and pepper

1 egg, lightly beaten

3oz (90g) medium oatmeal

5 teaspoons vegetable oil

1 onion, halved and sliced

1 pepper, red, green or yellow, cored, seeded and cut in strips

2oz (60g) mushrooms, sliced

1 tablespoon cornflour

¼ pint (150ml) stock

Exchanges per serving: Bread ¾
Fat 1¼
Protein 3¼
Vegetable ¾
25 Optional
Calories

1. Remove any sinews from the liver.
2. Season the flour with salt and pepper and transfer to a plate. Place the egg on a second plate and the oatmeal on a third plate.
3. Turn each slice of liver in the seasoned flour, the beaten egg and lastly the oatmeal. Put to one side.
4. Heat 1 teaspoon of oil in a large non-stick frying pan, add the onion and pepper and stir-fry for 3–4 minutes. Add the mushrooms and stir-fry for a further 1–2 minutes. Remove the vegetables with a slotted spoon.
5. Heat 2 teaspoons of oil in the pan, add as many slices of liver as possible and cook over a moderate heat until the underside is golden brown. Turn and cook the other side. Remove the liver from the pan, add the remaining oil and cook the rest of the oatmeal-coated liver in the same way. Remove from the pan.
6. Blend the cornflour and stock together, pour into the frying pan, add the vegetables and bring to the boil, stirring all the time. Add the liver, cover the pan and simmer for about 10 minutes or until the liver is cooked.

LAYERED COTTAGE PIE

Serves 4

405 Calories per serving

It's always worth buying extra lean minced beef. Cheap mince tends to have a high proportion of fat, so you're left with far less meat when it's been grilled.

1lb (480g) minced beef

1 teaspoon vegetable oil

1 onion, chopped

1 tablespoon flour

1 tablespoon tomato purée

4oz (120g) carrots, diced

3oz (90g) peas (approximately 6oz (180g) when bought in the pods)

9fl oz (270ml) beef stock

6oz (180g) spinach

1oz (30g) Cheddar, Double Gloucester or Red Leicester cheese, grated

For the topping:

1lb 2oz (540g) potatoes

salt

4 tablespoons skimmed milk

pepper

Exchanges per serving: Bread 1½
Fat ¼
Protein 3½
Vegetable 1¼
15 Optional Calories

1. Form the mince into small balls with dampened hands, place on a rack under a preheated grill and cook for 6–8 minutes, turning to brown all sides.
2. Heat the vegetable oil in a saucepan, add the onion and stir-fry for 3–4 minutes. Remove from the heat and stir in the flour.
3. Crumble in the minced beef, stir the tomato purée, carrots, peas and stock into the saucepan and bring to the boil, stirring all the time.
4. Meanwhile wash and roughly chop the spinach, transfer to a saucepan; cover and cook over a moderate heat for about 4 minutes. Drain well.
5. Spoon half the mince mixture into a deep ovenproof dish, spread the spinach over the mince, sprinkle with the cheese and spoon the remaining mince on top.
6. Boil the potatoes in salted water. Drain and mash with the milk; season to taste with salt and pepper.
7. Spread the potato over the mince and roughen the surface with a fork. Bake in a preheated oven, Gas Mark 5, 190°C, 375°F for 30–35 minutes until the potato has begun to turn golden brown.

VEGETABLE-TOPPED LAMB

Serves 4

260 Calories per serving

Remember to precook the lamb. It's surprising how much fat is lost during grilling.

For the base:

1lb (480g) minced lamb, crumbled

9oz (270g) aubergine

salt

7oz (227g) canned chopped tomatoes

1 small onion, chopped

2oz (60g) okra, halved

1 clove garlic, finely chopped

½ teaspoon rosemary

6 tablespoons water or weak stock

1 teaspoon cornflour

For the topping:

9oz (270g) swede, diced

9oz (270g) carrot, diced

salt

3 tablespoons single cream

good pinch of ground nutmeg

pepper

Exchanges per serving: Protein 3
Vegetable 3¼
30 Optional
Calories

1. Form the minced lamb into small balls with dampened hands, place on a rack under a preheated grill for 6–8 minutes, turning to brown all sides.
2. Cut the aubergine into cubes, place in a colander or sieve and sprinkle liberally with salt. Leave for about 20 minutes to allow time for the bitter juices to run out, then rinse well.
3. Place the aubergine, tomatoes, onion, okra, garlic, rosemary and 5 tablespoons of water or stock in a saucepan or flameproof casserole. Crumble the lamb into the mixture and bring to the boil, reduce the heat; cover and simmer for 20–25 minutes, stirring occasionally.
4. While the lamb is cooking, boil the swede and carrot in salted water for about 15 minutes, drain and transfer to a blender or food processor. Add the cream and seasonings and process until smooth.
5. Mix the cornflour to a paste with the remaining water or stock, add to the lamb and stir over a moderate heat for 1–2 minutes.
6. If the lamb has been cooked in a flameproof casserole, spread the carrot and swede purée on top and serve immediately. If the lamb has been cooked in a saucepan, transfer to a warm serving dish and spread the purée over the top.

FRANKFURTER BAKE

Serves 4

385 Calories per serving

The amount of vegetable oil used in this recipe keeps the bake crisp and light, but remember to preheat the oil and use the right size of tin.

For the batter:

4oz (120g) plain flour

pinch of salt

2 eggs, lightly beaten

¼ teaspoon English mustard

½ pint (300ml) skimmed milk

1 tablespoon grated Parmesan cheese

4 teaspoons vegetable oil

8oz (240g) frankfurters

Exchanges per serving:	Bread 1
	Fat 1
	Milk ¼
	Protein 2½
	10 Optional Calories

1. Sieve the flour and salt into a bowl, make a well in the centre, add the eggs and gradually beat or whisk in the mustard and milk. Alternatively, blend the ingredients in a blender or food processor until smooth. If time allows, put to one side for about 1 hour.
2. Spoon the oil into a 7-inch (18-cm) square baking tin about 2 inches (5 cm) deep. Cut the frankfurters into 2½-inch (6.5-cm) lengths and arrange them in the tin.
3. Transfer the tin to a preheated oven, Gas Mark 7, 210°C, 425°F for 5–7 minutes until the oil is very hot.
4. Stir the Parmesan cheese into the batter and quickly pour into the hot tin. Return the tin to the oven and bake for a further 40 minutes until well risen, brown and crisp. Serve immediately.

STUFFED MARROW RINGS

Serves 4

370 Calories per serving

This recipe can be served with vegetables or a tomato sauce and jacket potatoes.

1lb 4oz (600g) minced beef or lamb

approximately 2½lbs (1kg 100g) marrow

1 teaspoon vegetable oil

1 onion, finely chopped

½ teaspoon mixed herbs

2 tablespoons tomato purée

1oz (30g) fresh wholemeal or white breadcrumbs

2 eggs, beaten

salt and pepper

Exchanges per serving: Bread ¼
Fat ¼
Protein 4½
Vegetable 2½
5 Optional
Calories

1. Form the beef or lamb into small balls with dampened hands, place on a rack under a preheated grill and cook for 6–8 minutes, turning to brown all sides.
2. Cut a thin slice from each end of the marrow and cut the marrow into eight slices. Hollow out the centre of each slice, discarding all the seeds.
3. Heat the oil in a small pan, add the onion and stir-fry the crumbled minced meat for 3–4 minutes.
4. Place the minced beef in a bowl and mix in the onion, mixed herbs, tomato purée and breadcrumbs. Stir in the eggs and season well with salt and pepper.
5. Arrange the rings of marrow on a baking sheet lined with baking parchment or foil and pack the meat stuffing into each ring. Draw up the parchment or foil and fold over to seal. Bake in a preheated oven, Gas Mark 4, 180°C, 350°F for 1¼–1½ hours.

FRUIT CONDÉ

Serves 4

190 Calories per serving

This makes a refreshing change from hot rice pudding and you save fuel by cooking it on the hob. The rice mixture can be cooked the day before the pudding is to be served.

1 pint (600ml) skimmed milk

2oz (60g) short-grain or pudding rice

strip of lemon zest

2 tablespoons sugar

12oz (360g) fresh or drained canned pineapple rings or pieces

2 kiwi fruit, sliced

> **Exchanges per serving: Bread ½**
> **Fruit 1¼**
> **Milk ½**
> **30 Optional Calories**

1. Stir the milk, rice, lemon zest and sugar together in the top of a double saucepan or in a bowl which fits comfortably on top of a saucepan.
2. Bring the water in the saucepan to the boil and top with the rice mixture. Cover and leave over the simmering water for 1½–1¾ hours, or until the rice is cooked. Stir from time to time to prevent the rice from sticking together, and check that the water in the bottom saucepan doesn't boil dry.
3. Remove the rice from the heat and leave to cool. Chill if not required until the next day.
4. Discard the strip of lemon zest. Reserve some pineapple and a few slices of kiwi fruit for decoration, chop the remaining pineapple and transfer to four serving glasses with the kiwi fruit.
5. Spoon the cold rice over the fruit and decorate with the reserved pineapple and kiwi fruit.

BRAMBLE APPLE SEMOLINA

Serves 4

155 Calories per serving

To help prevent the colour of the blackberries from seeping into the semolina, use only a very small amount of water to stew the fruit. The semolina pudding can be used to top a variety of fruits such as cranberries and orange, blackcurrants and gooseberries.

1 medium cooking apple

5oz (150g) blackberries

1–2 tablespoons water

artificial sweetener to taste

½ teaspoon margarine

1 pint (600ml) skimmed milk

1½oz (45g) semolina

8 teaspoons sugar

Exchanges per serving: Bread ¼
Fruit ½
Milk ½
60 Optional
Calories

1. Peel, quarter and core the apple and slice thinly. Place the apple and blackberries with the water in a saucepan. Cover and simmer over a moderate heat for 8–10 minutes until the apple is tender. Sweeten to taste with artificial sweetener.
2. Grease a 1½-pint (900-ml) deep ovenproof dish with the margarine. Spoon the fruit into the greased dish.
3. Pour the milk into a saucepan and heat until steaming. Sprinkle the semolina and sugar into the milk and bring to the boil, stirring all the time. Boil for 4–5 minutes, stirring continuously until it begins to thicken.
4. Pour the semolina on top of the blackberry and apple and transfer to a hot oven, Gas Mark 6, 200°C, 400°F, for 25–30 minutes.

SAUCY PUDDING

Serves 4

225 Calories per serving

This light sponge pudding tops a delicious, moist sauce.

¼ teaspoon vegetable oil

2 tablespoons margarine

10 teaspoons caster sugar

finely grated zest and juice of 1 medium orange

finely grated zest and juice of ½ a lemon

2 eggs, separated

4fl oz (120ml) skimmed milk

2oz (60g) self raising flour, sieved

cream of tartar

1. Grease a 1½-pint (900-ml) ovenproof dish with the oil.
2. Gradually beat together the margarine and sugar. Add the zest and juice of the orange and lemon. Stir in the egg yolks, milk and flour and whisk well to form a smooth consistency.
3. Whisk the egg whites with a pinch of cream of tartar until peaking. Fold the fruit and milk mixture carefully into the egg whites using a metal tablespoon.
4. Transfer the mixture to the greased dish and bake at Gas Mark 4, 180°C, 350°F for about 35 minutes until puffy and golden brown. Serve immediately.

Exchanges per serving: Bread ½
Fat 1½
Fruit ¼
Protein ½
65 Optional
Calories

GOOSEBERRY PIE

Serves 4

255 Calories per serving

Gooseberries are in season when the elder trees are in flower, and a sprig of elderflowers gives gooseberries a lovely flavour. If you can't find elderflowers, add about half a teaspoon of ground cinnamon to the fruit.

For the pastry:

3oz (90g) wholemeal or plain flour

pinch of salt

8 teaspoons margarine

approximately 1 tablespoon ice-cold water

1 tablespoon wholemeal or plain flour for rolling out the pastry

For the filling:

15oz (450g) gooseberries, topped and tailed

1 sprig of elderflowers

5 tablespoons sugar

2 tablespoons water

> **Exchanges per serving: Bread ¾**
> **Fat 2**
> **Fruit ¾**
> **85 Optional Calories**

1. First of all, make the pastry. Stir the flour and salt together in a small bowl.
2. Add the margarine, which, if possible, has been stored in the freezer. Rub into the flour using the tips of your fingers and thumbs until the mixture resembles fresh breadcrumbs.
3. Using a round-bladed knife, mix the cold water into the pastry to form a dough. If time allows, wrap in clingfilm or foil and chill for 20–30 minutes.
4. Meanwhile place the gooseberries, elderflowers, sugar and water in a 1½-pint (900-ml) pie dish.
5. Sprinkle a sheet of non-stick baking parchment and a rolling pin with the remaining flour and roll out the pastry into a circle a little larger than the pie dish.
6. Cut a strip from all the way round the pastry, moisten the rim of the pie dish with a little water and press the strip of pastry onto it. Brush the pastry rim with a little water and cover with the pastry lid. Press the edges firmly together.
7. Trim the edges and press well together, flaking them with the back of a knife and scalloping in a decorative pattern.
8. If there are sufficient pastry trimmings, re-roll and cut leaves or decorative shapes to decorate the pie lid. Bake at Gas Mark 6, 200°C, 400°F for 15 minutes, then reduce the heat to Gas Mark 4, 180°C, 350°F for a further 20–30 minutes until the gooseberries are cooked.

JAMAICAN CRUMBLE

Serves 4

225 Calories per serving

The whole family will enjoy this crumble served hot, warm or cold with low-fat natural yogurt or cream.

For the crumble topping:

2oz (60g) wholemeal or plain flour

2 tablespoons margarine

½oz (15g) porridge oats

good pinch ground ginger

2 teaspoons soft brown sugar

4 teaspoons desiccated coconut

For the base:

juice of ½ a lemon

4 teaspoons soft brown sugar

6 tablespoons water

8oz (240g) fresh pineapple, cubed

8 lychees, stoned and halved

4 dates, stoned and halved

½ medium banana, sliced

Exchanges per serving: Bread ½
Fat 1½
Fruit 1½
55 Optional
Calories

1. First of all, make the crumble. Place the flour in a bowl and add the margarine, which, if possible, has been stored in the freezer. Rub into the flour until the mixture resembles fresh breadcrumbs. Stir in the porridge oats, ginger, sugar and coconut. Put to one side until the base has been prepared.
2. Place the lemon juice, sugar and water over a low heat until the sugar dissolves.
3. Mix all the prepared fruit together in a deep 5-inch (13-cm) ovenproof dish, pour over the syrup and sprinkle the crumble topping evenly over the fruit.
4. Bake in a preheated oven, Gas Mark 4, 180°C, 350°F for 35 minutes.

PLUM MERINGUE PIE

Serves 4

175 Calories per serving

The crushed digestive biscuits in the meringue make the topping wonderfully chewy and give it a delightful flavour.

12 medium dessert plums, halved and stoned

5 tablespoons water

artificial sweetener

2 egg whites

pinch of cream of tartar

6 tablespoons caster sugar

2 digestive biscuits, crushed

Exchanges per serving: Bread ½
Fruit 1½
100 Optional Calories

1. Gently heat the plums and water in a saucepan; cover and simmer very gently until the plums are just cooked but still retain their shape. Sweeten to taste with artificial sweetener and transfer to a deep ovenproof dish no more than 6½ inches (16.5cm) in diameter.
2. Whisk the egg whites and cream of tartar until peaking; gradually add the sugar, two tablespoons at a time and whisking well after each addition, until the mixture forms peaks again. Fold in the digestive crumbs.
3. Pile the digestive meringue on top of the plums and bake at Gas Mark 6, 200°C, 400°F for 15–20 minutes.

MANDARIN MERINGUE

Serves 4

220 Calories per serving

This recipe uses canned mandarins, but any other fruit canned in natural juice can be substituted.

For the base:

1oz (30g) cornflour

4 teaspoons caster sugar

½ pint (300ml) skimmed milk

6oz (180g) drained canned mandarins

2 egg yolks

For the meringue topping:

2 egg whites

pinch of cream of tartar

6 tablespoons caster sugar

Exchanges per serving: Bread ¼
Fruit ¼
Milk ¼
Protein ½
115 Optional
Calories

1. Blend the cornflour and sugar to a smooth paste with a little milk. Heat the remaining milk until steaming and gradually pour onto the cornflour paste, stirring all the time. Pour back into the saucepan and bring to the boil, stirring continuously.
2. Remove the saucepan from the heat and stir the mandarins and egg yolks into the sauce. Spoon into an ovenproof dish.
3. Whisk the egg whites and cream of tartar until peaking, then gradually whisk the sugar, 2 tablespoons at a time, into the egg whites and continue whisking until they peak again.
4. Pile the meringue on top of the mandarin sauce and bake at Gas Mark 5, 190°C, 375°F for 15–20 minutes.

AUTUMN PANCAKES

Serves 4

280 Calories per serving

Pancakes make a popular pudding at any time of the year, but filled with this plum and apple mixture they become very special.

For the filling:

8 medium plums

8oz (240g) cooking apples

2 tablespoons water

3 tablespoons sugar

1½ teaspoons arrowroot or cornflour

For the pancakes:

4oz (120g) plain flour

pinch of salt

1 egg, lightly beaten

½ pint (300ml) skimmed milk

1 tablespoon margarine or vegetable oil

Exchanges per serving: Bread 1
Fat ¾
Fruit 1½
Milk ¼
Protein ¼
50 Optional Calories

1. First of all, prepare the filling. Halve the plums, remove the stones and cut each plum into wedges. Quarter, core and peel the apples and slice thinly.
2. Place the fruit in a saucepan, add the water and sprinkle in the sugar. Cover the saucepan and cook the fruit over a low heat for 10–12 minutes or until cooked.
3. Drain the fruit and blend the juices with the arrowroot. Reheat the fruit juice and boil for 1 minute, then stir in the apple and plums and put to one side.
4. To make the pancakes, sieve the flour and salt into a bowl, make a well in the centre, add the egg and gradually beat or whisk in the milk.
5. Prove a 7-inch (18-cm) frying pan by generously sprinkling salt over the base, heating gently, tipping out the salt and wiping the pan thoroughly with kitchen paper. This will help prevent the pancakes sticking.
6. Heat a little margarine or oil in the pan and wipe again with kitchen paper.
7. Heat a little more margarine in the frying pan and pour in some batter, at the same time turning the pan so it thinly coats the base. Cook over a moderate heat until the underside is golden brown, then toss or turn over and cook the other side.
8. Transfer the cooked pancake to a plate; cover and keep warm in a low oven while repeating the procedure to make 15 or 16 pancakes.
9. Heat the fruit filling and place a spoonful on each pancake. Fold into quarters and serve immediately or keep warm for a short time in a low oven.

SOLO SPECIALS

There have been lots of requests for recipes suitable for one person – it's often difficult to adapt recipes designed for two or more – and this section is specifically devoted to meals for one, although the ingredients can easily be multiplied to feed a family or guests. If you frequently eat on your own, it's very easy to lose interest in the enjoyable aspects of preparing nutritious meals. It's possible these days to exist almost entirely on convenience foods, but they rapidly become monotonous and suppress the natural skills and imagination of the cook.

With the introduction of self-service greengrocers and greengrocery departments in supermarkets, shopping for one is no longer a problem. And if a recipe, like Kipper Salad (page 61), calls for half a red pepper, you can either use the other half in another recipe, for instance Pork and Vegetable Medley (page 67), or store it in the refrigerator, loosely covered by a plastic bag with holes pierced through like the ones supplied by most supermarkets. (With any fruit or vegetables which go brown when cut, brush the cut edges with lemon juice before storing.) If you need a lettuce, look out for the small varieties like 'Little Gem', or use the leftover leaves to make Lettuce Soup (page 53).

To save money on fuel bills, most of the recipes in this section make maximum use of the hob and grill, but dual ovens, with a conventional-sized oven and a small oven which doubles as a grill, make excellent economic sense – you can use the main oven for entertaining or cooking for the freezer and the small one for individual servings. Small portable ovens can sometimes be the answer for single cooks. Small quantities require suitable equipment, so invest in small saucepans, individual au gratin dishes and ramekins, etc.

There's no doubt that with a little careful shopping, the right equipment – and some help from this section! – cooking for one need never again be a chore.

LETTUCE SOUP

Serves 1

125 Calories per serving

So often when you make a salad there seems to be a great deal of lettuce left over. This soup is ideal for using up the tougher, outer leaves which are full of flavour. Some varieties of lettuce have naturally more flavour than others.

1 teaspoon margarine

½ medium onion, chopped

4oz (120g) lettuce leaves, shredded

4fl oz (120ml) weak stock

4 tablespoons skimmed milk

salt and pepper

lemon juice

good pinch ground allspice

1 tablespoon single cream

Exchanges per serving: Fat 1
Vegetable 2
55 Optional
Calories

1. Melt the margarine in a small saucepan, add the onion and stir-fry for 2–3 minutes. Stir in the lettuce, cover the pan and leave over a low heat for 2–3 minutes.
2. Stir in the stock, bring to the boil, reduce the heat; cover and simmer for 20 minutes.
3. Pour the lettuce, stock, etc. into a blender and process until smooth.
4. Transfer the lettuce soup to a clean saucepan, stir in the milk and season to taste with salt, pepper, lemon juice and allspice.
5. Reheat, stirring from time to time; pour into a warm bowl and swirl the single cream into the soup.

TOMATO AND NOODLE SOUP

Serves 1

155 Calories per serving

Tomatoes vary considerably in flavour — don't attempt to make this soup in the winter when they're bland and tasteless, wait until the summer when they are sweet, juicy and plentiful.

1 teaspoon margarine

½ medium onion, chopped

8oz (240g) tomatoes, roughly chopped

1 small carrot, roughly chopped

¼ pint (150ml) weak stock

sprig of fresh basil

salt and pepper

½oz (15g) vermicelli noodles

Exchanges per serving: Bread ½
Fat 1
Vegetable 3

1. Melt the margarine in a saucepan, add the onion and stir-fry for 3 minutes.
2. Stir in the tomatoes, carrot, stock and basil. Bring to the boil, reduce the heat, cover and simmer for 20 minutes.
3. Transfer the tomato mixture to a blender and process until smooth, sieve the purée by pressing the liquid through a sieve with the back of a spoon to extract all the juices.
4. Reheat the soup, adjust the seasoning and add the noodles; cover and simmer for about 5 minutes until the noodles are cooked.

CRISP-COATED COD

Serves 1

210 Calories per serving

If you're short of time yet want a nutritious meal, this recipe is ideal. It's quick to prepare and there's time to cook some vegetables to accompany it.

½oz (15g) fresh breadcrumbs

2 teaspoons chopped parsley

2 teaspoons grated Parmesan cheese

3½oz (105g) skinned tail-end cod fillet (or plaice, sole or other white fish)

2 teaspoons flour

2 teaspoons skimmed milk

1 teaspoon margarine

1. Mix together the breadcrumbs, parsley and Parmesan cheese.
2. Turn the cod in the flour, then the milk and lastly the breadcrumb mixture.
3. Melt the margarine and brush a small piece of foil, just large enough to hold the cod, with a little margarine.
4. Lay the cod on the foil and drizzle the remaining margarine over the top.
5. Place under a moderately hot grill for 10–12 minutes, turning once until the cod is cooked and golden brown.

Exchanges per serving: Bread ½
Fat 1
Protein 3
45 Optional
Calories

MINTY FISH

Serves 1

155 Calories per serving

The combination of white fish and a green minty sauce is not only delicious but looks attractive, too. Choose whichever fish you prefer or which suits your pocket – coley is much cheaper than sole, for example.

4-oz (120-g) white fish fillet, for example sole, plaice, cod, coley

3oz (90g) fresh or frozen peas

large pinch salt

sprig of mint

4 tablespoons skimmed milk

½–1 teaspoon lemon juice

salt and pepper

lemon wedge to serve

**Exchanges per serving: Protein 3
Vegetable 1
20 Optional
Calories**

1. Lay the fish on a piece of non-stick baking parchment in a steamer. Steam on top of the pan in which the peas will be cooked for 8–10 minutes, according to the size of the fillet.
2. Plunge the peas into salted boiling water with the sprig of mint and boil for about 10–12 minutes for fresh peas or 4–5 minutes for frozen peas.
3. Drain the peas and transfer, with the sprig of mint, to a blender. Add the milk and lemon juice and process until smooth.
4. Transfer the cooked fish fillet to a serving plate and keep warm.
5. Reheat the sauce and season to taste with salt, pepper and a little more lemon juice if necessary. Pour the hot sauce over the fish and serve with a wedge of lemon.

HADDOCK GRATINÉE

Serves 1

305 Calories per serving

Although I used smoked haddock for this recipe, smoked cod would be equally enjoyable. To make a complete meal, serve this gratinée with a crisp mixed salad.

4-oz (120-g) smoked haddock fillet

¼ pint (150ml) skimmed milk

1 teaspoon margarine

1 small onion, chopped

½ red pepper, seeded and cut into ½-inch (1.25-cm) squares

1 small courgette, roughly chopped

2 teaspoons cornflour

salt and pepper

1 tablespoon grated Parmesan cheese

Exchanges per serving: Fat 1
Milk ½
Protein 3
Vegetable 2
50 Optional Calories

1. Place the smoked haddock and milk in a saucepan; cover and simmer over a low heat for about 8 minutes until the haddock is cooked.
2. Using a fish slice, transfer the haddock to a plate, remove the skin and separate the fish into large flakes.
3. Melt the margarine, add the onion and stir-fry for 2–3 minutes. Add the pepper and stir-fry for a further 3 minutes; mix in the courgette and continue stirring for another 1–2 minutes.
4. Gradually blend the milk into the cornflour, pour into the vegetables and add the flaked fish. Season to taste.
5. Bring to the boil, stirring all the time. Boil for 1 minute. Remove from the heat and stir half the cheese into the mixture.
6. Transfer the haddock and vegetables to an au gratin dish, sprinkle with the remaining cheese and cook about 3 inches (7.5cm) away from a moderate grill for about 4 minutes until bubbling.

Top: Pear Snowball (p 84)
Bottom: Haddock Gratinée

MARINER'S MIX

Serves 1

350 Calories per serving

This three-layered mixture is full of flavour, and you don't need to use the whole oven — it's partially cooked on the hob and then browned under the grill.

¾ oz (25g) wholemeal or plain flour

2 teaspoons margarine

1 tablespoon grated Parmesan cheese

4oz (120g) skinned haddock fillet

½ small onion, finely chopped

4fl oz (120ml) mixed vegetable juice

1½ teaspoons cornflour

3oz (90g) young spinach leaves

Exchanges per serving:	Bread ¾
	Fat 2
	Fruit ½
	Protein 3½
	Vegetable 1
	45 Optional
	Calories

1. Place the flour in a small basin. Rub the margarine which, if possible, has been stored in the freezer, into the flour until the mixture resembles fresh breadcrumbs. Stir in the Parmesan cheese and put to one side while preparing the remaining ingredients.
2. Lay the haddock fillet in a small saucepan. Add the onion and vegetable juice; cover and simmer over a moderate heat for 8–10 minutes until the haddock is cooked.
3. Transfer the haddock to a plate and break the fish into large flakes.
4. Blend the cornflour to a paste with a little of the vegetable juice and pour back into the saucepan.
5. Wash the spinach, roughly chop and place it in a small saucepan; cover and cook over a low heat for 3–4 minutes. Drain well.
6. Bring the vegetable juice and onion to the boil, stirring all the time. Boil for 1 minute, then stir in the haddock.
7. Spread the spinach on the base of a warm, deep flameproof dish, about 4 inches (10 cm) in diameter. Spoon the haddock and vegetable juice mixture over the spinach and top with the Parmesan mixture.
8. Cook under a moderate grill for about 4 minutes until golden brown.

KIPPER SALAD

Serves 1

455 Calories per serving

By cooking the kipper fillet in the way described below, you save on washing up, but if you prefer, poach the fillet for 3–4 minutes in a frying pan or saucepan.

5-oz (150-g) kipper fillet

3oz (90g) potatoes, diced

salt

1½oz (45g) mangetout

½ small red pepper, seeded and cut in strips

4 teaspoons chopped spring onion

For the dressing:

2 teaspoons low-calorie mayonnaise

1 teaspoon lemon juice

1 tablespoon low-fat natural yogurt

To serve:

1 lemon wedge

1. Place the kipper fillet in a jug, cover with boiling water and leave in a warm place for 5–6 minutes. Drain.
2. Cook the potatoes in boiling salted water for about 10 minutes. Drain.
3. Boil the mangetout for 2–3 minutes in salted water. Drain.
4. Remove the skin from the kipper and flake the flesh into large pieces. Discard any small bones still attached to the fish.
5. Mix together the kipper, potatoes, mangetout, red pepper and spring onion.
6. Stir all the dressing ingredients together, spoon over the kipper salad and carefully mix through. Serve with a wedge of lemon.

Exchanges per serving: Bread 1
Fat 1
Protein 4
Vegetable 1
10 Optional
Calories

CURRIED PRAWNS

Serves 1

160 Calories per serving

The best curries in my opinion are the ones you make to suit your palate, which means using a variety of different spices and not a commercial curry powder – even though it may be more convenient. To help the spices retain their flavour, keep them in airtight containers in a dark cupboard. Try this recipe with long-grain rice which has been boiled with a good pinch of saffron.

3 cardamom pods

¼ teaspoon ground coriander

½ teaspoon ground cumin

¼ teaspoon cayenne

¼ teaspoon turmeric

1 teaspoon vegetable oil

½ teaspoon finely chopped fresh ginger

½ clove garlic, crushed

1 shallot or small onion, chopped

2 teaspoons tomato purée

5 tablespoons water

3oz (90g) peeled prawns

sprigs of fresh coriander to garnish (optional)

1. Split the cardamom pods, remove the seeds and lightly crush them with the back of a tablespoon.
2. Mix the cardamom seeds, coriander, cumin, cayenne and turmeric together.
3. Heat the vegetable oil in a small saucepan, add the ginger and garlic and stir over a low heat for 1 minute. Do not allow the ginger to burn.
4. Add the onion to the saucepan and stir-fry for 3–4 minutes. Stir in the spices.
5. Blend the tomato purée and water together, add to the onion and spices, mix in the prawns and bring to simmering point over a low heat. Simmer for 5–7 minutes, stirring occasionally. Decorate with sprigs of fresh coriander and serve with brown or saffron rice.

Exchanges per serving: Fat 1
Protein 3
Vegetable ½
10 Optional
Calories

CHICKEN FRUIT GRILL

Serves 1

205 Calories per serving

This simple but interesting dish is a good way of using up leftover canned fruit.

5-oz (150-g) skinned chicken breast on the bone

2oz (60g) drained canned pineapple, reserving 2 tablespoons of the juice

1 teaspoon chopped mint

1 teaspoon lemon juice

1 teaspoon margarine

Exchanges per serving: Fat 1
Fruit ½
Protein 3½

1. Place the chicken breast in a non-metallic dish.
2. Mix together the reserved pineapple juice, mint and lemon juice, pour over the chicken and leave to marinate for 1½ hours, turning occasionally.
3. Drain the marinade from the chicken and lay bone-side uppermost on a grill rack. Dot with a little margarine and grill under a moderate to hot heat for 5 minutes. Turn the chicken, dot with the remaining margarine and grill for a further 4 minutes.
4. Transfer the chicken to an au gratin dish and pour over the marinade. Finely chop the pineapple and add to the dish. Return to the grill and cook for a further 3–4 minutes, basting the chicken with the marinade. Serve at once.

CHICKEN LAYER BAKE

Serves 1

175 Calories per serving

This recipe is cooked in foil, which reduces the washing up! Remember to keep the shiny side of the foil inside – this reduces the cooking time.

3-oz (90-g) skinned and boned chicken breast

1-oz (30-g) slice of cooked ham

2oz (60g) carrot

1 small courgette

salt

1 tablespoon spring onion

¼–½ teaspoon tarragon

pepper

4 teaspoons white wine

Exchanges per serving: Protein 3
Vegetable 1½
20 Optional
Calories

1. Cut lengthways through the chicken breast. Fold the ham in half, place on top of the bottom half of the chicken, then place the other half of the chicken on top of the ham. Secure the three layers together with two cocktail sticks.
2. Cut the carrot into matchstick-sized strips. Slice the courgette.
3. Plunge the carrot and courgette into boiling salted water and boil for 3–4 minutes. Drain well.
4. Lay a piece of foil, about 8 inches (20cm) square, on a baking sheet. Place the carrot, courgette and spring onion in the centre, lay the chicken on top and sprinkle with the tarragon, salt and pepper and wine.
5. Fold the edges of the foil over to make a parcel and bake in a preheated oven, Gas Mark 4, 180°C, 350°F for 20–25 minutes.
6. Open the foil package, transfer the vegetables and chicken to a serving plate, remove the cocktail sticks and serve.

CHEESY SALSIFY

Serves 1

420 Calories per serving

This recipe can be made with either variety of salsify – the white variety, otherwise known as oyster plant, or the black-skinned scorzonera. To make a complete meal, serve the salsify with a crisp mixed salad.

4oz (120g) salsify

1½ teaspoons lemon juice

large pinch salt

1½ teaspoons margarine

1 tablespoon chopped onion or shallot

1 tablespoon flour

¼ pint (150ml) skimmed milk

pinch powdered mustard

2oz (60g) cheese, e.g. mature Cheddar or Double Gloucester, grated

salt and pepper

1 tomato

Exchanges per serving: Fat 1½
Milk ½
Protein 2
Vegetable 2½
30 Optional
Calories

1. Peel or scrape the salsify and immediately place in a bowl of cold water with about a teaspoon of lemon juice. This prevents it discolouring.
2. Cut the salsify into 3-inch (7.5-cm) lengths and boil in salted water with about ½ teaspoon lemon juice until tender, about 20 minutes.
3. Melt the margarine in a small saucepan, add the onion and stir-fry for 3–4 minutes. Stir in the flour and remove from the heat.
4. Gradually blend in the milk; return to the heat and bring to the boil, stirring all the time. Boil for 1–2 minutes. Stir in the mustard, about 1½oz (45g) cheese and season to taste with salt and pepper.
5. Drain the salsify and place in a flameproof dish, pour over the hot cheese sauce and sprinkle with the remaining cheese. Cook under a preheated hot grill until bubbling.
6. Cut the tomato into wedges or slices, arrange on top of the salsify and grill for a further 1–2 minutes until the sauce is golden and the tomato warm. Serve immediately.

PORK AND VEGETABLE MEDLEY

Serves 1

270 Calories per serving

Served with plain boiled rice, this recipe makes a filling meal. It's a useful way of using up leftover vegetables – parsnip or swede can be prepared in the same way and used instead of carrot.

3oz (90g) pork fillet

1½ teaspoons vegetable oil

½ teaspoon fresh ginger, chopped

½ onion, finely chopped

½ red or yellow pepper, seeded and cut into thin strips

3oz (90g) carrot, cut in matchstick-sized pieces

3oz (90g) courgette, cut in matchstick-sized pieces

4 tablespoons stock

2 teaspoons tomato purée

1 tablespoon soy sauce

salt and pepper

1. Place the pork on a rack under a preheated grill and cook, turning once, until the fat has stopped dripping from the meat. Set aside.
2. Heat the oil in a saucepan, add the ginger, onion and pepper and stir-fry for 3–4 minutes.
3. Remove the saucepan from the heat and stir in the carrot and courgette.
4. Cut the pork into thin strips, add to the saucepan, return to a moderate heat and stir round for 1–2 minutes.
5. Stir in the stock, tomato purée and soy sauce. Cover the saucepan and simmer for 8–10 minutes, stirring occasionally. Season with salt and pepper.

Exchanges per serving: Fat 1½
Protein 2½
Vegetable 3
10 Optional
Calories

PARMA PARCEL

Serves 1

225 Calories per serving

There can be very few meals which are as quick as this one. It takes longer to prepare the salad or cook the vegetables to accompany the main recipe!

1oz (30g) Parma ham (weighed when all fat has been removed)

2oz (60g) cottage cheese

2oz (60g) curd cheese

2oz (60g) fresh or drained canned pineapple, chopped

dash hot pepper sauce

few chicory or endive leaves

Exchanges per serving: Fruit ½
Protein 3

1. Lay the slice of Parma ham out flat. If you have more than one slice, overlap them slightly to make a single rectangle.
2. Mix together the cottage and curd cheeses, add the pineapple and season with a dash of hot pepper sauce.
3. Spoon the cheese mixture into the Parma ham and fold the ham over to cover the cheese.
4. Arrange the chicory or endive leaves on a serving plate and place the parma parcel on top.

SAVOURY HIDDEN SANDWICH

Serves 1

425 Calories per serving

Choose a cheese to suit your taste. I prefer a mild cheese and find that Gorgonzola, for example, tends to dominate the flavour of the ham.

2 × 1-oz (30-g) slices bread

2 × ¾-oz (20-g) slices cooked ham

¾oz (20g) cheese, sliced or grated

2 teaspoons chopped spring onions

1 egg

1 tablespoon skimmed milk

salt and pepper

1 teaspoon vegetable oil

Exchanges per serving: Bread 2
Fat 1
Protein 3¼
5 Optional
Calories

1. Place the bread on a work surface and cover each slice with a slice of ham.
2. Mix the grated cheese with the spring onion and spread on one slice of ham. If using sliced cheese, lay it on the ham and sprinkle over the spring onions. Cover with the other slice of ham and bread.
3. Lightly beat the egg and milk together on a shallow plate and season with salt and pepper.
4. Turn the sandwich several times in the egg until it is totally absorbed.
5. Heat the oil in a small non-stick frying pan until beginning to smoke; lower the heat and add the sandwich. Fry until the underside is golden brown, then turn and fry the other side. Serve immediately.

Ham-wrapped Endive

Serves 1

180 Calories per serving

Instead of heating the oven for just one meal, I wrapped the endive in ham and simmered them very gently in orange juice. The result was a great success! You can very easily double or treble the ingredients to serve a family or guests.

2 endive, approximately 3½oz (105g) each

2 × 1-oz (30-g) slices cooked smoked gammon

1 teaspoon margarine

4 teaspoons finely chopped onion

1 medium orange

Exchanges per serving:	Fat 1
	Fruit 1
	Protein 2
	Vegetable 2½

1. Trim the endive and wash well, keeping the heads whole.
2. Wrap each endive in a slice of gammon and put to one side.
3. Melt the margarine in a small heavy-based saucepan, add the onion and stir-fry for 3–4 minutes. Remove from the heat.
4. Lay the ham and endive on top of the onion, squeeze the juice from the orange and pour it into the saucepan. Bring to the boil, cover and reduce the heat to as low as possible. Do not add salt to the recipe as there is sufficient in the gammon. Simmer for 35–40 minutes.

SAVOURY CHILLI BEEF

Serves 1

415 Calories per serving

This recipe is fairly mild but if you'd like a hotter version, more like a chilli con carne, add a little chilli powder or some crushed chillies to the tomatoes.

4oz (120g) minced beef

1 teaspoon vegetable oil

1 small clove garlic, crushed

½–¾ chilli, seeded and finely chopped

1 small onion, chopped

2 teaspoons flour

1 small can chopped or whole tomatoes (227g)

½ green or red pepper, seeded and cut in half rings

3oz (90g) drained canned kidney beans

salt and pepper

1 teaspoon chopped parsley

Exchanges per serving: Bread 1
Fat 1
Protein 3
Vegetable 4
20 Optional
Calories

1. Form the mince into small balls with dampened hands, place on a rack under a preheated grill and cook for 6–8 minutes, turning to brown all sides.
2. Heat the oil in a saucepan, add the garlic, chilli and onion and stir-fry for 3–4 minutes.
3. Sprinkle in the flour and gradually blend in the tomatoes. If using canned whole tomatoes, break them up with a wooden spoon while stirring the mixture. Crumble in the mince and bring to the boil, stirring continuously. Cover, reduce the heat and simmer for 20 minutes, stirring from time to time to prevent the mince sticking to the base of the saucepan.
4. Add the green or red pepper and kidney beans to the saucepan; cover and simmer for a further 10 minutes.
5. Adjust the seasoning, adding salt and pepper to taste. Sprinkle with parsley and serve.

BEEFBURGER

Serves 1

375 Calories per serving

This beefburger needn't be served in a bap. It can be eaten with a mixed salad or a selection of hot vegetables.

5oz (150g) minced beef

good pinch mixed herbs

salt and pepper

1½-oz (45-g) sesame seed bap

½ teaspoon margarine

2 small lettuce leaves

few slices of onion

1 gherkin, sliced lengthways

1 small tomato, sliced

Exchanges per serving: Bread 1½
Fat ½
Protein 4
Vegetable 1

1. Mix the beef and herbs together; season with salt and pepper.
2. Shape the beef into a pattie about the same size as the sesame seed bap and grill for 10–15 minutes, turning once.
3. Halve the bap and spread with the margarine.
4. Arrange the lettuce on the bottom half of the bap and top with the onion rings. Place the hot beefburger on top of the onion and arrange the gherkin and tomato on top of the beefburger. Cover with the other half of the bap and serve immediately.

VEAL WITH CREAMY COURGETTE SAUCE

Serves 1

270 Calories per serving

When you feel like treating yourself, try this recipe. It's quick and easy to prepare – just the thing when you want to relax after a busy day.

4-oz (120-g) veal escalope

1 teaspoon lemon juice

For the sauce:

1 teaspoon margarine

1 shallot, finely chopped

1½oz (45g) courgette, cut in matchstick-sized pieces

2 teaspoons water

2 teaspoons lemon juice

3 tablespoons single cream

salt and pepper

1. Sprinkle one side of the veal with half the lemon juice and put to one side.
2. Make the sauce. Melt the margarine in a small saucepan, add the shallot and stir-fry for 3 minutes.
3. Add the courgette, water and lemon juice; cover and continue cooking over a moderate heat for 5–6 minutes, stirring occasionally.
4. Meanwhile, place the veal on a rack under a preheated grill and cook for 4 minutes. Turn, sprinkle with the remaining lemon juice and continue cooking for 4–5 minutes.
5. Remove the lid from the saucepan, stir in the cream and season with salt and pepper. Heat gently.
6. Transfer the veal to a warm plate and pour over the hot creamy sauce.

Exchanges per serving: Fat 1
Protein 3
Vegetable 1
100 Optional
Calories

SPINACH-TOPPED LAMB

Serves 1

275 Calories per serving

This meal is easy and quick to prepare and cook. Serve with a mixed salad or, alternatively, tomatoes which can be grilled at the same time as the lamb, and 3oz (90g) sweetcorn. Remember to add 1 Bread Exchange if you have sweetcorn.

4½-oz (135-g) lamb leg steak

For the topping:

3oz (90g) fresh spinach

1 tablespoon single cream

1 teaspoon chopped chives

salt and pepper

good pinch freshly grated nutmeg

1 teaspoon grated Parmesan cheese

Exchanges per serving: Protein 3
Vegetable 1
45 Optional
Calories

1. Grill the lamb steak under a moderate grill for 10–12 minutes, turning once.
2. Prepare the topping. Wash the spinach well, shake off the excess water and chop the leaves. Transfer to a heavy-based saucepan, cover and bring to the boil. The leaves should hold sufficient water to cook the spinach but, if necessary, add 2 teaspoons of water. Boil for 3–4 minutes until tender. Drain well, pressing out any liquid.
3. Mix together the chopped spinach, single cream, chives, salt, pepper and nutmeg.
4. Spread the hot spinach mixture over the lamb steak, sprinkle with the grated Parmesan cheese and return to the grill for a further 1–2 minutes.

SPICED KIDNEYS IN YOGURT

Serves 1

280 Calories per serving

Plain boiled noodles or rice accompany this dish well. If you add to the recipe 1oz (30g) noodles or rice, boiled in salted water, remember to add 1 Bread Exchange.

1oz (30g) back bacon

2 × 2-oz (60-g) lamb's kidneys

1 teaspoon flour

salt and pepper

1½ teaspoons vegetable oil

2 tablespoons chopped spring onions

½ teaspoon ground coriander

½ teaspoon ground cumin

1½oz (45g) small mangetout

2oz (60g) mushrooms, sliced

2 tablespoons stock

2½ tablespoons low-fat natural yogurt

Exchanges per serving: Fat 1½
Milk ¼
Protein 4
Vegetable 1½
10 Optional
Calories

---

1. Grill the bacon; chop and put to one side.
2. Remove the skin from the kidneys, cut in half lengthways and cut out the white cores.
3. Season the flour with salt and pepper and turn the kidney halves in the seasoned flour.
4. Heat 1 teaspoon of oil in a small saucepan, add the kidneys and brown over a moderate heat. Remove the kidneys from the saucepan.
5. Add the remaining oil, spring onions, coriander and cumin and stir-fry for 1–2 minutes. Add the mangetout and mushrooms and stir-fry for a further 2 minutes.
6. Mix the bacon, kidneys, together with any juices which have run from them, and stock in the saucepan and stir well. Cover the saucepan and simmer for 8–10 minutes. Remove the lid from the saucepan and continue cooking over a lower heat for a further 10 minutes, stirring from time to time.
7. Allow the kidneys to cool a little, stir in the yogurt and serve.

LIVER WITH ORANGE

Serves 1

305 Calories per serving

This delicious combination is also excellent nutritionally. The Vitamin C in the orange helps the body absorb the iron in the liver.

4oz (120g) lamb's liver

1 medium orange

1½ teaspoons margarine

½ onion, chopped

1 teaspoon chopped parsley

Exchanges per serving: Fat 1½
Fruit 1
Protein 3
Vegetable ½

1. Cut the liver into thin strips and put to one side.
2. Cut the orange in half lengthways. Cut the zest and pith from one half, divide it into segments and remove as much of the membrane as possible. Squeeze the juice from the other half.
3. Heat the margarine in a frying pan, add the onion and stir-fry for 2 minutes. Add the liver and stir-fry for a further 3–4 minutes.
4. Pour the orange juice into the pan and stir well. Simmer for 3–4 minutes, then add the orange segments and heat through.
5. Spoon the liver and orange into a serving bowl or onto a plate and sprinkle with parsley.

RHUBARB AND ORANGE JELLY

Serves 1

75 Calories per serving

Instead of serving the jelly with frozen whipped dessert topping, you can eat it on its own or with low-fat natural yogurt.

6oz (180g) rhubarb

1 medium orange

artificial sweetener

2 teaspoons gelatine

1 tablespoon frozen whipped dessert topping

Exchanges per serving: Fruit 1
                                    35 Optional
                                    Calories

1. Cut the rhubarb into 1½-inch (4-cm) lengths and place in a saucepan.
2. Remove a little of the orange zest with a zester, wrap in clingfilm and put to one side. Squeeze the juice from the orange.
3. Pour the orange juice into the saucepan with the rhubarb. Place over a moderate heat and cover and simmer for a few minutes until the rhubarb is cooked.
4. Transfer the rhubarb and orange to a blender and process until smooth. Sweeten to taste with the artificial sweetener and sprinkle the gelatine into the hot purée, stirring all the time. Leave until the gelatine has dissolved.
5. Pour the purée into a glass or mould and leave until set.
6. If the jelly has been set in a mould, dip the mould briefly in hot water before turning out onto a serving plate.
7. Spoon the frozen whipped dessert topping on top of the jelly and sprinkle with the reserved orange zest.

CHEESE-TOPPED APRICOTS

Serves 1

120 Calories per serving

Like some cheesecakes, this simple dessert has a very mild cheese flavour. The topping can be used over a variety of fresh or drained canned fruits.

For the base:

2 medium apricots

2 teaspoons sherry

For the topping:

1oz (30g) curd cheese

2 tablespoons low-fat natural yogurt

1½ teaspoons caster sugar

few drops of almond essence

Exchanges per serving: Fruit 1
Protein ½
60 Optional
Calories

1. Cut the apricots in half, remove the stones and roughly chop the flesh. Place in a ramekin and sprinkle with sherry.
2. Beat the curd cheese, yogurt, ½ teaspoon sugar and a few drops of almond essence together.
3. Spoon the topping over the fruit and sprinkle the remaining sugar evenly over the top.
4. Place the ramekin under a preheated grill for a few minutes until golden and bubbling. Serve warm or chilled.

OAT-TOPPED CURRANTS

Serves 1

240 Calories per serving

I love fruit crumbles, so if I'm cooking for myself I make this oat-topped mixture which is quickly prepared and browned under the grill.

For the topping:

½oz (15g) wholemeal flour

½oz (15g) porridge oats

1 teaspoon sugar

2 teaspoons margarine

For the fruit base:

5oz (150g) mixed red and blackcurrants

1 tablespoon water

artificial sweetener to taste

Exchanges per serving: Bread 1
Fat 2
Fruit 1
20 Optional
Calories

---

1. Begin by preparing the topping. Stir the flour, porridge oats and sugar together. Rub the margarine which, if possible, has been stored in the freezer, into the flour until the mixture resembles fresh breadcrumbs. Put to one side.
2. Place the currants and water in a small saucepan and simmer gently until cooked. Sweeten to taste with artificial sweetener.
3. Transfer the hot cooked currants to a warm flameproof ramekin, about 3½ inches (9cm) in diameter.
4. Sprinkle the topping over the currants and place under a preheated moderate grill for about 2 minutes until golden brown and crisp.

PRUNE AND APRICOT COMPÔTE

Serves 1

165 Calories per serving

This is a very refreshing dessert which is delicious at any time of the year. Serve it on its own, or with frozen dessert topping and a little lemon zest as suggested below.

3 medium dried prunes

1oz (30g) dried apricots

½ a lemon

2 teaspoons honey

large pinch allspice

2 tablespoons frozen whipped dessert topping

Exchanges per serving: Fruit 2
70 Optional Calories

1. Cover the prunes and apricots with cold water and leave for several hours.
2. Place the fruit in a small saucepan and add 4 tablespoons of water, including the liquid the fruit has been soaking in.
3. Remove the zest from the lemon half with a zester or grater, cover with clingfilm and put in the refrigerator. Squeeze the juice.
4. Add the lemon juice, honey and allspice to the fruit; place over a moderate heat and simmer for 10–12 minutes.
5. Spoon the compôte into a serving dish and serve hot, warm or chilled. Before serving, top with the frozen whipped dessert topping and sprinkle with the reserved lemon zest.

SUMMER CUP

Serves 1

125 Calories per serving

There are several different types of cantaloupe melon. I chose a Charentais, but I could have used a rock or Ogen. The skin from the melon acts as an attractive container for the fruit salad.

For the salad:

½ **medium Charentais melon**

2oz (60g) **cherries**

2½oz (75g) **raspberries**

½ **teaspoon caster sugar**

For the topping:

2 **tablespoons low-fat natural yogurt**

1 **teaspoon caster sugar**

Exchanges per serving: Fruit 2
50 Optional
Calories

1. Scoop out and discard the melon seeds. Using a teaspoon or melon baller, carefully remove as much flesh as possible and place the flesh in a bowl with any juice which escapes.
2. Stone the cherries and add to the melon.
3. Add the raspberries and ½ a teaspoon of caster sugar to the melon and cherries; mix well. Spoon the fruit into the melon skin and chill until required.
4. Mix the yogurt and caster sugar together. Just before serving, pour over the sweetened yogurt.

PEAR SNOWBALL

Serves 1

210 Calories per serving

This dessert is best eaten with a knife and fork as the meringue is soft, but the pear and dates remain fairly firm. Choose a really juicy, ripe pear for this recipe.

1 medium pear

2 fresh dates, stoned

1 small egg white (size 5)

pinch of cream of tartar or salt

2 tablespoons caster sugar

finely grated zest of ¼ of a lemon

Exchanges per serving: Fruit 2
140 Optional Calories

1. Remove the core from the pear, but do not peel yet or it will go brown. Reserve the bottom ½-inch (1.25-cm) of the core and replace in the bottom of the pear.
2. Chop the dates and fill the pear cavity.
3. Whisk the egg white, cream of tartar and 1 tablespoon of sugar until the mixture peaks, then whisk in the remaining sugar and lemon zest. Keep whisking until the mixture peaks again.
4. Peel the pear and place on an ovenproof plate. Spread the meringue all over the pear and onto the plate, drawing the meringue into peaks.
5. Bake in a preheated oven, Gas Mark 6, 200°C, 400°F for 10–12 minutes. Lay the ovenproof dish and pear on a larger plate and serve.

FRUIT WHIP

Serves 1

120 Calories per serving

Instead of apricots you can use other fruits which are available, but always use the banana as it thickens the purée. If you wish to use kiwi fruit, sieve the mixture – don't use a processor as it will split the tiny black seeds and the mixture will taste bitter.

2 medium apricots

½ medium banana

1 teaspoon lemon juice

1 teaspoon sugar

5 tablespoons low-fat natural yogurt

2–3 drops almond essence

ground cinnamon

1. Plunge the apricots in boiling water and leave for about 1 minute. Peel off the skins, halve them, remove the stones and roughly chop the flesh.
2. Slice the banana and place with the apricot, lemon juice, sugar, yogurt and almond essence in a blender and process until smooth.
3. Pour the fruit purée into a serving glass, sprinkle with a little ground cinnamon and chill until ready to serve.

> **Exchanges per serving: Fruit 2**
> **Milk ½**
> **20 Optional**
> **Calories**

MANDARIN JUNKET

Serves 1

90 Calories per serving

Junket has been made for many hundreds of years. Always use fresh skimmed milk, not long life, or the essence of rennet will not cause the milk to set. This is an ideal dessert to prepare while your main course is cooking as it only takes 15–20 minutes to set at room temperature.

2oz (60g) well-drained canned mandarin segments

¼ pint (150ml) skimmed milk

1 teaspoon honey or sugar

¾ teaspoon essence of rennet

few drops of orange flower water or vanilla essence

pinch of ground cinnamon

1. Place the mandarin segments in a serving dish.
2. Heat the milk and honey or sugar until luke-warm, but do not allow to boil. If you want to be really accurate, use a thermometer and heat to 37°C, 100°F. Remove from the heat.
3. Stir the essence of rennet, flavouring and cinnamon into the milk. Pour the milk over the mandarins and leave undisturbed at room temperature for 15–20 minutes until set.

> **Exchanges per serving: Fruit ½**
> **Milk ½**
> **20 Optional**
> **Calories**

CREAM-TOPPED FLUMMERY

Serves 1

125 Calories per serving

This dessert is simple to make for one person but is easily adapted to feed two or more. It tastes and looks attractive so it's an ideal sweet for a lunch or dinner party.

1 medium peach

½ medium grapefruit

2 teaspoons arrowroot or cornflour

1 teaspoon sugar

1 tablespoon soured cream

½ teaspoon desiccated or shredded coconut, toasted

Exchanges per serving: Fruit 2
80 Optional
Calories

1. Halve the peach, remove the stone and roughly chop the flesh. Place in a blender.
2. Squeeze the juice from the grapefruit, add it to the peach and process to form a purée.
3. Press the purée through a sieve to remove any skin and lumps of flesh.
4. Blend the arrowroot or cornflour with a little of the fruit purée and stir into the rest of the purée, add the sugar, bring to the boil and boil for 1 minute, stirring all the time.
5. Pour the fruit into a wine glass or narrow dessert glass, leave to cool and then chill until ready to serve.
6. Spread the soured cream over the top of the fruit and sprinkle with the toasted coconut.

CREAMY PAPAYA

Serves 1

110 Calories per serving

This creamy dessert is simple to make and a treat to eat. The lime complements the papaya and adds a slight tang.

½ medium papaya

1 teaspoon lime juice

1 teaspoon caster sugar

2 tablespoons single cream

slice of lime

Exchanges per serving: Fruit 1
85 Optional
Calories

1. Scoop out and discard the black seeds from the centre of the papaya.
2. Remove the flesh from the papaya and place in a blender (there isn't enough for a food processor); add the lime juice, caster sugar and cream and process until smooth. If you don't possess a blender, mash the papaya until smooth, then gradually blend in the remaining ingredients.
3. Transfer the creamed papaya purée to a serving glass and chill until required. Serve with a slice of lime to decorate the papaya on the edge of the glass.

BANANA IN RAISIN SAUCE

Serves 1

95 Calories per serving

The raisins must be left for at least 2 hours in the orange juice so that they swell and absorb some of the juice. Serve this dessert with low-fat natural yogurt or single cream, but remember to add the extra Calories.

½oz (15g) raisins

juice of ½ a medium orange

½ medium banana

1 teaspoon lemon juice

½ teaspoon clear honey

Exchanges per serving: Fruit 2
10 Optional
Calories

1. Soak the raisins in the orange juice for 2–3 hours.
2. Slice the banana and toss in the lemon juice.
3. Place the raisins, orange juice and honey in a saucepan over a low heat, bring to the boil and simmer for 1–2 minutes.
4. Pour the hot sauce over the bananas and serve warm or chilled.

GINGER FRUIT SALAD

Serves 1

150 Calories per serving

The tangy syrup used in this recipe combines well with the flavour of pears and bananas, but is equally good with other fruits such as kiwi fruit and lychees.

juice of ½ a lemon

½ medium banana

1 medium pear

½ teaspoon finely chopped fresh ginger

1 tablespoon caster sugar

4 tablespoons water

**Exchanges per serving: Fruit 2
60 Optional
Calories**

1. Squeeze the juice from the lemon; pour half into a dish and the remainder into a small saucepan.
2. Peel the banana and cut in diagonal slices. Stir into the dish containing the lemon juice.
3. Peel the pear or, if you prefer, leave the skin on. Cut it in quarters and remove the core. Cut each quarter into three slices, transfer to the dish and turn to coat in lemon juice – this prevents the fruit from discolouring.
4. Add the ginger, sugar and water to the saucepan and heat gently until the sugar has dissolved, then boil uncovered for 1–2 minutes. Pour the syrup over the fruit and leave to cool. Serve cold.

No Cook

The recipes in this section include starters, snacks, salads, main courses, desserts and drinks, but not one of them has to be baked, grilled or boiled. The most you have to do is to melt margarine or dissolve gelatine!

Chilled soups like Gazpacho (page 90), and other dishes liked Piped Peaches (page 97) and Summer Pudding (page 114) can be prepared well in advance – particularly convenient if you're planning a complicated main dish and need all the time you can get.

There are a wide variety of imaginative salads and some of them, like the Smoked Tofu Salad (page 102), can be made to look very attractive and colourful indeed. A selection of salads will make a meal in itself, or serve one or two with a hot main dish.

Children love to help in the kitchen, and you can let them try their hand at some of these cold dishes without the fear of them burning themselves. And there's the added bonus that by allowing them to prepare fresh, nutritious ingredients, they'll be encouraged towards a lifelong preference for healthy food.

Suitable at all times of the year and for any occasion – picnics, packed lunches and buffets – these wonderfully simple recipes are designed to rescue you from the 'hot stove' once in a while, and still your family and guests will come back for more!

GAZPACHO

Serves 4

25 Calories per serving

This low-calorie version of the traditional Spanish soup is quickly and simply made using a blender or food processor.

8fl oz (240ml) mixed tomato and vegetable juice

9oz (270g) tomatoes, roughly chopped

1 clove garlic, chopped

1 small onion, chopped

½ large red pepper, seeded and chopped

½ large green pepper, seeded and chopped

1 tablespoon red wine vinegar

1½ teaspoons chopped basil

2oz (60g) cucumber, chopped

salt and pepper

4 sprigs of basil

1. Place the tomato and vegetable juice, tomatoes, garlic, onion, red and green peppers, wine vinegar, chopped basil and cucumber in a blender or food processor and process until smooth.
2. Season to taste with salt and pepper; chill well.
3. To serve, pour the soup into four bowls and garnish each serving with a sprig of fresh basil.

Exchanges per serving: Fruit ¼
Vegetable 1¼

STUFFED DATES

Serves 4
200 Calories per serving

When friends come for drinks in the evening, these make a welcome change from the inevitable bowls of crisps and nuts.

4oz (120g) curd cheese

3 tablespoons peanut butter, smooth or crunchy

¾oz (20g) large raisins

2 tablespoons low-fat natural yogurt

2 teaspoons finely grated orange zest

20 fresh dates

1. Beat the curd cheese and peanut butter together.
2. Roughly chop the raisins and add to the cheese mixture with the yogurt and orange zest.
3. Slit each date lengthways, remove the stone and spoon a little of the stuffing into each date. Arrange on a serving plate.

Exchanges per serving: Fat ¾
Fruit 2
Protein 1¼
40 Optional Calories

CHEESY PINEAPPLE BALLS

Serves 6
100 Calories per serving

These savouries are ideal for serving with drinks.

3oz (90g) fresh pineapple

4oz (120g) Danish blue cheese

4oz (120g) curd cheese

approximately 2 tablespoons chopped chives

1. Cut the pineapple into twelve cubes.
2. Crumble the Danish blue cheese into a bowl and mash with a fork. Gradually mix in the curd cheese.
3. Divide the cheese into twelve and roll each cube of pineapple in the cheese mixture to form twelve balls.
4. Roll six of the pineapple balls in the chopped chives. Chill well before serving.

Exchanges per serving: Protein 1
5 Optional Calories

CHILLED CUCUMBER SOUP

Serves 4

45 Calories per serving

A chilled soup makes a refreshing start to a summer lunch or dinner. This soup can be prepared well in advance and stored in the refrigerator, but stir well before serving.

1 large cucumber

10fl oz (300ml) low-fat natural yogurt

4 teaspoons chopped salad burnet or chervil

2 teaspoons chopped chives

1 clove of garlic

salt and pepper

Exchanges per serving: Milk ½
Vegetable 1

1. Cut a few thin slices from the cucumber, wrap them in clingfilm and reserve for garnishing the soup.
2. Lightly peel the cucumber so the skin is removed but the green-coloured flesh remains intact. Cut the cucumber in half lengthways, scoop out and discard the seeds.
3. Roughly chop the cucumber and place in a blender or food processor, add the yogurt, salad burnet and chives and process until smooth. Chill well.
4. Before serving, rub the peeled clove of garlic round each serving bowl, season the soup with salt and pepper and pour into the four bowls. Garnish with the reserved cucumber slices and serve.

AVOCADO DIP

Serves 4

110 Calories per serving

Serve this dip with a variety of crudités: carrot, celery, pepper and cucumber sticks and halves of mushrooms and radish. If the dip is prepared in advance, push the avocado stone below the surface of the mixture to slow down the browning process, then remove just before serving.

½ avocado

1 tablespoon lemon juice

4 teaspoons chopped chives

2oz (60g) cottage cheese

4oz (120g) curd cheese

salt

dash of pepper sauce

lemon slices

Exchanges per serving: Protein ¾
50 Optional
Calories

1. Scoop the avocado flesh into a blender, scraping the skin to obtain the light green colour.
2. Add the lemon juice, chives and cottage and curd cheeses; process until smooth. Season to taste with salt and pepper sauce.
3. Spoon the avocado dip into a small serving bowl and garnish with lemon slices.

SIMPLE LIVER PÂTÉ

Serves 3

185 Calories per serving

This simple pâté is very quick to make. The only 'cooking' involved is the heating of the vegetable stock to dissolve the gelatine!

5 tablespoons weak vegetable stock

½ teaspoon gelatine

4oz (120g) liver sausage

4oz (120g) curd cheese

2 tablespoons chopped spring onions

1 tablespoon brandy

salt and pepper

2 radishes

Exchanges per serving: Protein 2
10 Optional
Calories

1. Heat the vegetable stock until steaming and pour into a small cup or basin. Sprinkle in the gelatine and stir well. Stand the cup or basin in a saucepan of simmering water and leave until the gelatine has completely dissolved.
2. Place the liver sausage, curd cheese, spring onions, brandy and 3 tablespoons of the vegetable stock and gelatine into a blender. Process until smooth. Season to taste with salt and pepper.
3. Transfer the liver pâté to a small dish; smooth and level the top.
4. Thinly slice the radishes and arrange on top of the pâté.
5. When the remaining vegetable stock begins to set, spoon it carefully over the radishes and pâté to seal the surface.

ANCHOVY TOMATOES

Serves 2

120 Calories per serving

These tomatoes may be served as an appetiser or as part of a buffet meal or snack.

2 tomatoes

4oz (120g) curd cheese

2 teaspoons low-calorie mayonnaise

4 anchovy fillets, chopped

1 teaspoon chopped basil

2 stuffed olives, sliced

few chicory or lettuce leaves

> **Exchanges per serving: Fat ½**
> **Protein 1**
> **Vegetable 1**
> **15 Optional**
> **Calories**

1. Cut the tomatoes in half. Scoop out the seeds and place in a sieve to catch the juice from the tomatoes.
2. Beat together the curd cheese, mayonnaise and 1 tablespoon of tomato juice. Stir in the chopped anchovy fillets and basil.
3. Either spoon the anchovy cheese filling back into each tomato half, or transfer to a piping bag fitted with a ½-inch (1.25-cm) nozzle and pipe the filling back into the tomato halves.
4. Arrange the sliced stuffed olives on top of each tomato half and transfer to two serving plates. Garnish each plate with a few whole or shredded chicory or lettuce leaves.

Piped Peaches

Serves 4

60 Calories per serving

Serve these peaches as a starter for four people, or as a snack for two with a selection of salads. Remember to adjust the Exchanges accordingly.

2 medium peaches or nectarines

1 teaspoon lemon juice

1oz (30g) cooked ham

2 teaspoons chopped chives

3oz (90g) curd or quark cheese

salt

dash of pepper sauce

4 sprigs of parsley

few endive leaves

**Exchanges per serving: Fruit ½
Protein ½
5 Optional
Calories**

1. Halve the peaches, discard the stones and, using a teaspoon, scoop out some of the peach flesh leaving sufficient for the peach halves to retain their shape. Brush each half with the lemon juice.
2. Finely chop the scooped out peach and ham; mix together with any remaining lemon juice.
3. Mix together the chopped peach, ham, chives and cheese; season with salt and pepper sauce.
4. Pipe the cheese mixture back into each peach half and place a sprig of parsley on top.
5. Lay endive leaves on each serving plate and place a peach half on each plate.

CHEESE-FILLED PEARS

Serves 2

360 Calories per serving

This delightful recipe is suitable for any occasion. Use really ripe pears and brush them well with lemon juice to prevent them turning brown.

For the filling:

4oz (120g) Gorgonzola cheese

4oz (120g) curd cheese

4 teaspoons chopped chives

2 teaspoons lemon juice

2 tablespoons low-fat natural yogurt

2 medium pears

lemon juice

a few radicchio or chicory leaves

Exchanges per serving: Fruit 1
Protein 3
10 Optional
Calories

1. First of all, make the filling. Mash the Gorgonzola cheese with a fork, add the curd cheese and mash once again to mix. Gradually add the chives, lemon juice and yogurt.
2. Cut the pears in half lengthways and scoop out the core using a teaspoon. Brush the cut edges of the pears with lemon juice.
3. Spoon the cheese filling into a piping bag fitted with a ½-inch (1.25-cm) star nozzle and pipe the filling over the cut edges of the pears, filling the hole left by the core. Alternatively, spoon the filling on top of the pears.
4. Arrange the radicchio or chicory leaves on the serving dishes, place the pear halves on top and serve.

ITALIAN-STYLE SALAD

Serves 4

160 Calories per serving

This salad has a strong flavour so serve it with other, milder salads and warm crusty bread. Red leafed lettuces make this salad look very attractive, so look out for them when they're in season.

lettuce or chicory leaves

3 tomatoes

2–3oz (60–90g) cucumber

4oz (120g) Mozzarella cheese

2oz (60g) Parma ham

6 anchovy fillets, rinsed under cold water

4 black olives, stoned and quartered

For the dressing:

4 teaspoons red wine vinegar

1 teaspoon chopped basil

2 teaspoons olive oil

pinch of powdered mustard

Exchanges per serving: Fat ½
Protein 1½
Vegetable 1
15 Optional
Calories

1. Arrange the lettuce or chicory leaves round the edge of the serving bowl or plate.
2. Cut the tomatoes into thin wedges or slices. Slice the cucumber and cut the cheese into ½-inch (1.25-cm) cubes. Place in a mixing bowl.
3. Cut the Parma ham into thin strips. Cut the anchovy fillets in half lengthways, then in half again. Add the ham, anchovy fillets and black olives to the mixing bowl.
4. Place all the dressing ingredients in a small, screw-top jar and shake well, or whisk all the ingredients together in a small basin.
5. Pour the dressing over the ingredients in the mixing bowl, tossing gently to coat. Spoon the dressed salad into the centre of the lettuce or chicory-lined serving dish.

MIXED SALAD

Serves 4

30 Calories per serving

This low-calorie mixed salad with a tangy dressing is delicious served with hot or cold meats or fish. It's well worth including the chive flowers if they are available – they add an attractive and unusual colour to the salad.

For the salad:

1 radicchio

1 green pepper, cored, seeded, halved and sliced

1 yellow pepper, cored, seeded, halved and sliced

4oz (120g) fennel, sliced

1 medium orange

2 chive flowers, if available

For the dressing:

4 tablespoons buttermilk

1 tablespoon lemon juice

2 tablespoons chopped chives

salt and pepper

Exchanges per serving: Fruit ¼
Vegetable 1½
5 Optional
Calories

1. Separate the radicchio leaves; mix together with the green and yellow peppers and fennel.
2. Using a sharp knife, remove the peel and white pith from the orange. Cut in between each membrane and remove the whole orange segments, catching and reserving any juice which drips from the orange during preparation. Stir the orange segments into the radicchio salad.
3. Place the reserved orange juice and all the dressing ingredients in a small screw-top jar and shake well to mix. Alternatively, place all the ingredients in a small bowl and whisk together.
4. Pour the dressing over the salad and toss well. Separate the chive petals and sprinkle over the salad.

Tofu-dressed Salad

Serves 4

75 Calories per serving

This salad is ideal for vegetarians and non-vegetarians alike. Serve it with a selection of other salads at a barbecue, or pack in a suitable container to take on a picnic. It looks particularly attractive with the red-tinged lettuces such as Lollo Rosso.

For the salad:

few lettuce or radicchio leaves

2–3oz (60–90g) cucumber, sliced

2 kiwi fruit, sliced

1 yellow pepper, cored, seeded and sliced

6 radishes, sliced

3oz (90g) fennel, sliced

For the dressing:

6oz (180g) soft or silken tofu

½ teaspoon fresh chopped ginger

2 tablespoons lemon juice

1 teaspoon soy sauce

2 teaspoons olive oil

salt and pepper

1. Arrange the lettuce or radicchio leaves around the edge of the salad bowl or plate.
2. Mix together all the other salad ingredients and spoon into the centre of the arranged leaves.
3. Place the tofu, ginger, lemon juice, soy sauce and olive oil in a blender and process until smooth. Season to taste with salt and pepper.
4. Transfer the dressing to a small bowl and serve separately, or spoon over the centre of the salad and mix well.

Exchanges per serving: Fat ½
Fruit ½
Protein ½
Vegetable 1

SMOKED TOFU SALAD

Serves 2

105 Calories per serving

Smoked tofu has a distinctive flavour, but it can be hard to find. Ask in good quality delicatessen and health food stores.

1 radish

few endive leaves

2 tomatoes, sliced

2-inch (5-cm) wedge of cucumber, sliced

6oz (180g) smoked tofu

few sprigs of watercress

For the dressing:

2 teaspoons olive oil

1 tablespoon lemon juice

2 teaspoons chopped chives

salt and pepper

Exchanges per serving: Fat 1
Protein 1
Vegetable 2

1. Trim the leaf, if still attached, and the root from the radish. Using a sharp knife, cut through from the root end to the base, but keep the radish base joined. Make 6–8 cuts through the radish, then place in very cold water for at least an hour to allow time for the radish to open out into a water-lily shape.
2. Arrange the endive leaves round the edge of a serving plate about 9 inches (22.5cm) in diameter.
3. Arrange the tomato, then the cucumber in rings.
4. Cut the smoked tofu into ½-inch (1.25-cm) cubes and pile in the centre of the plate. Decorate with the sprigs of watercress and the radish water-lily.
5. To make the dressing, place all the dressing ingredients in a small, screw-top jar and shake well to mix. Alternatively, whisk together in a small bowl. Spoon the dressing over the salad.

TABBOULEH

Serves 4

135 Calories per serving

The bulgar wheat used in this Middle Eastern dish is sold under many different names such as burghul, pourgouri or cracked wheat. As it has already been partially cooked it only requires soaking before use.

4oz (120g) bulgar (cracked) wheat

½ pint (300ml) boiling water

½ mild onion, finely chopped

1 red, green or yellow pepper, or a mixture, cored, seeded and chopped

1 tablespoon chopped mint

1 tablespoon chopped coriander

For the dressing:

2 teaspoons tomato purée

1 tablespoon olive oil

1 tablespoon lemon juice

½ teaspoon ground cumin

½ teaspoon ground coriander

salt and pepper

Exchanges per serving: Bread 1
Fat ¾
Vegetable ½
5 Optional
Calories

1. Place the bulgar wheat in a bowl, pour over the boiling water and leave for 25–30 minutes. Spoon the bulgar into a clean cloth and squeeze well to drain off all the excess water.
2. Mix together the bulgar, onion, pepper, mint and coriander.
3. Place all the dressing ingredients in a screw top jar and shake well to mix. Alternatively, whisk all the ingredients together in a small basin.
4. Pour the dressing over the salad and mix well.

TUNA AND WHEAT SALAD

Serves 3

165 Calories per serving

This salad is ideal for an everyday lunch or supper, but it's also a popular buffet dish, accompanied by a selection of other salads.

3oz (90g) bulgar (cracked) wheat

8fl oz (240ml) boiling water

½ red pepper, seeded and finely chopped

8 black olives, stoned and halved

3 tablespoons chopped spring onions

4oz (120g) well drained canned tuna, flaked

4 teaspoons chopped parsley

For the dressing:

4 teaspoons low-calorie mayonnaise

1 tablespoon lemon juice

salt and pepper

1. Place the bulgar wheat in a bowl, pour over the boiling water and leave for 25–30 minutes. Spoon the bulgar into a clean cloth and squeeze well to drain off all the excess water.
2. Mix together the bulgar, red pepper, olives, spring onions, tuna and parsley.
3. Stir the mayonnaise and lemon juice together in a small basin or cup and season well with salt and pepper.
4. Spoon the dressing over the salad and stir thoroughly to coat all the ingredients.

> **Exchanges per serving: Bread 1**
> **Fat ½**
> **Protein 1¼**
> **Vegetable ¼**
> **35 Optional**
> **Calories**

SMOKED MACKEREL SALAD

Serves 2

260 Calories per serving

I prefer the peppered smoked mackerel for this salad, but if you aren't keen on its strong flavour, substitute plain smoked mackerel. As the fish is fairly oily and mixed with tangy fruits, the salad doesn't require a separate dressing.

1 medium apple

2 teaspoons lemon juice

1 medium orange

3oz (90g) Chinese leaves, shredded

1 small bulb fennel, thinly sliced

1 stick celery, chopped

3 or 4 radishes, sliced

6oz (180g) peppered smoked mackerel fillets, skinned

a few sprigs of watercress

Exchanges per serving: Fruit 1
Protein 3
Vegetable 1½

1. Cut the apple into quarters, remove the core, slice thinly and toss in the lemon juice.
2. Using a sharp knife, remove the peel and white pith from the orange and cut between each membrane to remove the segments.
3. Mix together the apple, orange segments, Chinese leaves, fennel, celery and radishes.
4. Flake the mackerel into fairly large pieces and add to the salad.
5. Transfer the salad to a serving plate and garnish with several sprigs of watercress.

CUCUMBER FRUIT SALAD

Serves 4

60 Calories per serving

This unusual combination is delicious with grilled fish or meat. It can be prepared in advance, covered and kept in the refrigerator.

½ medium Galia melon

5-oz (150-g) wedge of water melon

3oz (90g) black grapes, halved and seeded

6oz (180g) cucumber

For the dressing:

1 tablespoon olive oil

2 tablespoons wine or cider vinegar

1 tablespoon chopped chives

salt and pepper

Exchanges per serving: Fat ¾
Fruit ¾
Vegetable ½

1. Remove the seeds from the Galia melon, peel away the skin and cut the flesh into cubes, approximately ¾ inch (2cm) in size.
2. Remove the skin from the water melon, cut into cubes the same size, removing the black seeds while preparing the fruit.
3. Mix the Galia and water melon cubes together and add the black grapes.
4. Cut the cucumber into cubes, approximately the same size as the melon and add to the fruit.
5. Place all the dressing ingredients in a small, screw-top jar and shake well to mix. Alternatively, whisk the ingredients together in a small basin.
6. Pour the dressing over the salad and toss well.

SAVOURY PEAR SALAD

Serves 2

235 Calories per serving

This refreshing salad combines several different flavours and textures. If the salad is prepared in advance, the flavour isn't affected but the pear gradually absorbs the strong colour of the beetroot.

1½oz (45g) watercress

3oz (90g) Edam cheese

2 tablespoons chopped spring onions

6oz (180g) freshly cooked beetroot

1 medium pear

1 teaspoon lemon juice

For the dressing:

1 tablespoon lemon juice

1½ teaspoons olive oil

¼ teaspoon Dijon mustard

salt and pepper

Exchanges per serving: Fat ¾
Fruit ½
Protein 1½
Vegetable 2¼

1. Break the sprigs of leaves off the top of the watercress and roughly chop the coarse stalk.
2. Cut the cheese into strips measuring about ¼ inch × 1½ inches (5mm × 4cm).
3. Mix together the watercress, cheese and spring onions.
4. Remove the skin from the beetroot and cut into pieces roughly the same size as the cheese. Stir into the salad bowl.
5. Peel the pear, cut in quarters and remove the core. Cut into pieces roughly the same size as the cheese and beetroot. Immediately toss the prepared pear in the lemon juice, to prevent it discolouring, then stir in with the other salad ingredients.
6. Place all the dressing ingredients into a small, screw-top jar and shake well to mix, or whisk them together in a small bowl. Pour the dressing over the salad and serve.

SPICED FRUIT SALAD

Serves 4

65 Calories per serving

Use top quality fruit for this recipe. The melon should smell fragrant and 'give' slightly when pressed.

For the syrup:

juice of ½ a lemon

4½ teaspoons clear honey

4 tablespoons water

2 cardamom pods

2 cloves

2-inch (5-cm) stick of cinnamon

For the salad:

½ medium cantaloupe melon such as Galia, Ogen or rock

4 medium apricots

6 fresh dates

> **Exchanges per serving: Fruit 1½**
> **25 Optional**
> **Calories**

1. Place the lemon juice, honey and water in a saucepan. Open the cardamom pods and add the seeds from the pods to the saucepan with the cloves and cinnamon. Bring the syrup to the boil over a low heat and simmer for 2–3 minutes. Leave to cool a little while preparing the salad.
2. Either shape the melon into balls using a melon baller or teaspoon, or cut into cubes.
3. Halve the apricots, remove the stones and cut each half into four wedges.
4. Cut the dates in half lengthways, remove the stones and cut each half to form quarters.
5. Mix all the fruit together, pour over the syrup and chill until ready to serve.

CHICKEN AND PRAWN SALAD

Serves 4

245 Calories per serving

This salad served with jacket potatoes makes a wonderfully satisfying meal. If you wish, you can reduce the amount of chicken you use and increase the prawns.

10oz (300g) cooked chicken, cubed

4oz (120g) peeled prawns

8 black olives, stoned and halved

½ medium papaya

½ medium pink grapefruit, cut lengthways

1oz (30g) sprigs of watercress

4 radishes, sliced

½ avocado

a few endive, chicory, radicchio or lettuce leaves

For the dressing:

1 tablespoon olive oil

2 tablespoons lemon juice

2 tablespoons chopped spring onions

salt and pepper

1. Mix together the chicken, prawns and olives.
2. Discard the round black seeds from the papaya, peel away the skin and cut the flesh into cubes.
3. Separate the grapefruit into segments and remove as much of the membrane as possible, catching any juice which may escape.
4. Stir the papaya, grapefruit, watercress and radishes into the chicken mixture.
5. Remove the peel from the avocado, slice the flesh thinly and stir into the chicken salad.
6. Place the reserved grapefruit juice with all the dressing ingredients in a small, screw-top jar and shake well to mix. Alternatively, whisk all the ingredients together in a small basin.
7. Pour the dressing over the salad and stir carefully to coat all the ingredients.
8. Arrange the endive leaves round the edge of a serving plate or bowl and spoon the salad into the centre.

Exchanges per serving: Fat ¾
Fruit ½
Protein 3½
Vegetable ¼
60 Optional
Calories

Top: Strawberry Ripple *(p 121)*
Bottom: Chicken and Prawn Salad

HAM AND TURKEY RING

Serves 4

80 Calories per serving

This is an interesting way of serving leftover cold meats. It's particularly useful at Christmas or Easter if you have a large quantity of turkey left over and want to serve it in an unusual way.

¾ pint (450ml) vegetable stock

1 tablespoon gelatine

3oz (90g) cucumber

3oz (90g) cooked ham, diced

3oz (90g) cooked turkey, diced

a few endive, radicchio or lettuce leaves

3 tomatoes, cut into wedges

sprigs of watercress

> **Exchange per serving: Protein 1½**
> **Vegetable 1**

1. Heat 4 tablespoons of the stock until steaming and pour into a small basin or cup. Sprinkle in the gelatine and stir well. Stand the basin or cup in a saucepan of simmering water and leave until the gelatine has dissolved.
2. Place a 1½-pint (900-ml) ring mould in the refrigerator to chill.
3. Stir the dissolved gelatine mixture into the remaining stock. Spoon a little of the stock into the ring mould and return to the refrigerator until set.
4. Thinly slice the cucumber. When the stock in the ring mould has almost set, arrange some of the cucumber slices attractively in the setting stock. Return to the refrigerator until the rest of the stock is thick and beginning to set.
5. Spoon a little of the setting stock over the cucumber and cover with a layer of the ham and turkey, spoon over some more stock and refrigerate for a few minutes.
6. Cover with a second layer of cucumber and stock, then turkey and ham and stock. If there is sufficient cucumber, arrange the remaining slices on top and cover with the remaining stock. Chill well for about 3 hours.
7. To serve, dip the mould quickly in hot water, cover with the serving plate and turn upside down. Remove the mould. Decorate the ham and turkey ring with the endive, radicchio or lettuce leaves. Pile the tomato wedges in the centre and garnish with sprigs of watercress.

MIXED FRUIT AMBROSIA

Serves 2

115 Calories per serving

This dessert is quick to make in a blender or food processor and keeps well in the refrigerator. I leave the peach skin on, but if you prefer, remove it before blending.

½ medium mango

½ medium banana

1 medium peach or nectarine

5oz (150g) strawberries

1 tablespoon caster sugar

1 teaspoon lemon juice

2 teaspoons sherry

1 grape (optional), halved and seeded

Exchanges per serving: Fruit 2
35 Optional
Calories

1. Remove the skins from the mango and banana, roughly chop the fruit and place in a blender or food processor.
2. Cut the peach in half, remove the stone, roughly chop the fruit and add to the mango and banana.
3. Reserve three small strawberries, roughly chop the remainder and transfer to the blender. Add the sugar, lemon juice and sherry. Process until smooth.
4. Pour the mixture into two dessert glasses and chill.
5. Halve each of the reserved strawberries and decorate each dessert with half a grape and three strawberry halves.

SUMMER PUDDING

Serves 4

200 Calories per serving

This is a traditional British pudding which can be made with a selection of berries, like the ones given here, or with black, red and white currants which will need to be cooked first.

15oz (450g) mixture of raspberries, loganberries, tayberries and blackberries

6 tablespoons caster sugar

5oz (150g) thin crustless slices of wholemeal or white bread

Exchanges per serving: **Bread 1¼**
Fruit ¾
90 Optional Calories

1. Wash the fruit and place in a bowl, sprinkle with the sugar and stir to mix evenly. Leave for about an hour until the juices begin to flow from the berries.
2. Line a 1-pint (600-ml) pudding basin with the bread, slightly overlapping the joins and leaving sufficient to cover the top.
3. Spoon the fruit and its juices into the lined basin. Cover with the remaining bread and lay a plate or saucer slightly smaller than the basin on top of the pudding. Place several weights on top of the plate and chill overnight or for at least six hours. It is a good idea to transfer the weighted basin to a large plate to catch any juices which may run from the pudding.
4. To serve, invert the pudding onto the serving plate, remove the basin and cut into four wedges.

STRAWBERRY AND ORANGE RING

Serves 4

90 Calories per serving

This tangy dessert is simple enough to make for a family meal, and because it's so attractive it's ideal when you're entertaining friends.

16fl oz (480ml) orange juice

2 tablespoons caster sugar

4 teaspoons gelatine

juice of 1 lemon

5oz (150g) strawberries

Exchanges per serving: Fruit 1¼
30 Optional
Calories

1. Heat 4fl oz (120ml) of orange juice and the sugar until the sugar has dissolved. Remove the steaming orange juice from the heat and stir in the gelatine. Leave until completely dissolved.
2. Stir the gelatine into the remaining orange juice and add the lemon juice.
3. Pour a little of the orange mixture into a 1½-pint (900-ml) ring mould. Transfer the ring mould to the refrigerator.
4. Halve the strawberries.
5. When the jelly in the ring mould has set, arrange half the strawberries on top and pour a little more orange mixture over them. Return the mould to the refrigerator but leave the remaining orange mixture at room temperature.
6. Remove the jelly from the refrigerator and arrange the remaining strawberries on top, pour over the remaining orange mixture and chill for several hours or overnight.
7. To serve, dip the ring mould quickly in hot water and invert onto a serving plate.

LEMON AND SULTANA CHEESECAKE

Serves 4
265 Calories per serving

The ideal tin for this recipe is a 6-inch (15-cm) loose-bottomed flan tin with a small base and sloping sides about 1½ inches (4cm) high, but as these are not readily available, I tested the recipe in a 6-inch (15-cm) cake tin and although the crumb base was a little thin it worked well.

For the base:

3 large digestive biscuits

4 teaspoons margarine

For the topping:

zest and juice of ½ a lemon

1oz (30g) sultanas

3oz (90g) cottage cheese

3oz (90g) curd cheese

5 tablespoons caster sugar

5fl oz (150ml) low-fat natural yogurt

2 tablespoons hot water

1 tablespoon gelatine

1 large egg white (size 1 or 2)

pinch of cream of tartar

For decoration:

thin slices of lemon

Exchanges per serving:	
	Bread ¾
	Fat 1
	Fruit ¼
	Milk ¼
	Protein ¾
	80 Optional Calories

1. Finely grate the zest from the lemon and wrap in clingfilm. Squeeze the juice from the lemon half and leave the sultanas soaking in the lemon juice while preparing the other ingredients.
2. Place the biscuits in a plastic bag and crush with a rolling pin to make fine crumbs. Melt the margarine and stir in the biscuit crumbs. Mix well, then press firmly into a 6-inch (15-cm) loose-bottomed cake tin or flan tin.
3. Beat together the cheeses, lemon zest and caster sugar; gradually add the yogurt.
4. Pour the hot water into a cup or small basin; sprinkle in the gelatine and stir well. Stand the cup in a saucepan of simmering water and leave until the gelatine has completely dissolved.
5. Stir the dissolved gelatine, sultanas and lemon juice into the cheese mixture and leave until beginning to set.
6. Whisk the egg white and cream of tartar until peaking. Using a metal spoon, fold the egg white evenly into the cheese mixture, then spoon over the biscuit base and chill until completely set.
7. To serve, remove the base from the cake or flan tin, then slide a spatula or palette knife under the biscuit base and slide the cheesecake onto the serving plate. Decorate with the lemon slices.

RHUBARB FOAM

Serves 2

65 Calories per serving

The early forced rhubarb, which is a pinky red, gives this recipe a very pretty colour. Older rhubarb tends to give it a less appealing green tinge.

8oz (240g) young pink rhubarb

1 medium orange

artificial sweetener

2 teaspoons gelatine

2oz (60g) quark cheese

1 egg white

pinch of cream of tartar

Exchanges per serving: Fruit ½
Protein ½
10 Optional
Calories

1. Cut the rhubarb into 1-inch (2.5-cm) lengths and place in a saucepan.
2. Squeeze the juice from the orange, add half to the rhubarb and pour the remainder into a cup.
3. Gently heat the rhubarb and orange; simmer for 8–10 minutes. Sweeten to taste with the artificial sweetener and leave to cool.
4. Sprinkle the gelatine into the orange juice in the cup and stir well. Place the cup in a saucepan of simmering water and leave until the gelatine has completely dissolved.
5. Spoon the cheese into a blender or food processor, add the rhubarb and process until smooth. Pour into a bowl, stir in the dissolved gelatine and leave until beginning to set.
6. Whisk the egg white and cream of tartar until peaking and fold into the setting rhubarb mixture. Spoon into two serving dishes and refrigerate until completely set.

FIG FIESTA

Serves 2

135 Calories per serving

Fresh figs are a luxury well worth buying. Wait until they're in season and don't buy the shrivelled fruit so often displayed on supermarket shelves.

2 large figs

5oz (150g) strawberries

1 kiwi fruit, sliced

2½ teaspoons caster sugar

4 teaspoons Marsala or sweet sherry

2 tablespoons single cream

Exchanges per serving: Fruit 2
70 Optional
Calories

1. Cut the figs in half, then cut each half into three or four wedges.
2. Cut the strawberries in half or, if they're very big, slice them thickly.
3. Mix the three fruits together and sprinkle with the sugar and Marsala. Leave to marinate for 2 hours, carefully stirring from time to time to coat the fruit in the Marsala.
4. Spoon the fruit into two dishes and divide the juices evenly between each serving. Pour a tablespoon of cream over the fruit and serve immediately.

BLUEBERRY DREAM

Serves 4

80 Calories per serving

You can make this dessert in advance and keep it chilled until ready to serve. The fruit purée is thick enough to hold the blueberries evenly through the mixture, so they won't sink to the bottom!

½ medium mango

½ medium papaya

½ medium banana

5fl oz (150ml) low-fat natural yogurt

juice of ½ a lime

4 teaspoons clear honey

5oz (150g) blueberries

4 slices of lime for garnish

Exchanges per serving: Fruit 1
Milk ¼
20 Optional
Calories

1. Scrape the mango flesh from the skin and around the stone; place in a food processor or blender.
2. Scoop out and discard the black seeds from the papaya, peel off the skin, roughly chop the flesh and add to the mango.
3. Peel and roughly chop the banana; add to the mango and papaya.
4. Add the yogurt, lime juice and honey to the fruit and process until smooth.
5. Pour the fruit purée into a bowl and stir in the blueberries. Spoon into four glasses or dishes and chill until ready to serve. Garnish with slices of lime.

SUNFLOWER SALAD

Serves 4

80 Calories per serving

This simple dessert is ideal for every day, yet refreshing and attractive enough for a dinner party.

4 tablespoons apple juice

2 teaspoons honey

½ medium banana

1 medium apple or pear, or half of each

2 teaspoons lemon juice

2 medium clementines

3oz (90g) green or black grapes, or a mixture

4 teaspoons sunflower seeds, toasted

4 sprigs of mint

1. Place the apple juice and honey in a small saucepan and heat gently until the honey dissolves. Put to one side to cool.
2. Peel and slice the banana. Quarter the apple or pear, remove the core and slice the fruit. Toss the banana and apple or pear in the lemon juice.
3. Peel the clementines and separate into segments.
4. Halve the grapes and remove any pips.
5. Mix all the fruits together and pour over the syrup.
6. Spoon the salad into four serving bowls and sprinkle over the toasted sunflower seeds. Garnish with a sprig of mint and chill for an hour before serving.

Exchanges per serving: Fruit 1
35 Optional
Calories

STRAWBERRY ICE CREAM SHAKE

Serves 1

110 Calories per serving

This is always popular, with adults as well as children. You can increase the amount of ice cream by 1oz (30g), either by adding it to the blender or scooping it in just before serving, but if you do this, remember to increase the Optional Calories to 120.

2½oz (75g) strawberries

1oz (30g) vanilla or strawberry ice cream

5 tablespoons skimmed milk

1 teaspoon caster sugar

1. Place all the ingredients in a blender and process until smooth and frothy. Serve immediately.

Exchanges per serving: Fruit ½
Milk ¼
70 Optional
Calories

STRAWBERRY RIPPLE

Serves 2

150 Calories per serving

This dessert is simple to make and refreshing to eat. Strawberries are now available most of the year but in my opinion, they taste best when they're freshly picked.

10oz (300g) strawberries

3 tablespoons caster sugar

2 tablespoons water

2½ teaspoons gelatine

4 tablespoons low-fat natural yogurt

1. Reserve one or two strawberries for decoration and place the remainder in a blender or food processor with the sugar. Process until smooth.
2. Pour the water into a cup or small basin and sprinkle in the gelatine. Stand the cup in a saucepan of simmering water and leave until completely dissolved.
3. Stir the dissolved gelatine into the strawberry purée and leave until beginning to set.
4. Add the yogurt, but do not stir evenly into the setting purée. White streaks should remain.
5. Spoon the mixture into two serving glasses and refrigerate until set. Before serving, decorate with whole, halved or sliced strawberries.

Exchanges per serving: Fruit 1
110 Optional
Calories

TROPICAL SALAD

Serves 4

120 Calories per serving

This combination of tropical fruit is accompanied by a sharp, slightly sweetened sauce.

For the salad:

1 lime

4 teaspoons sugar

1 teaspoon orange flower water

6 tablespoons water

½ medium papaya

½ medium banana

4 lychees

1½oz (45g) black grapes, halved and seeded

4 dates, stoned and halved

1 kiwi fruit, sliced

For the sauce:

4 tablespoons soured cream

4 tablespoons low-fat natural yogurt

1 teaspoon clear honey

> **Exchanges per serving: Fruit 1½**
> **70 Optional**
> **Calories**

1. Remove the zest from the lime with a zester, wrap a few strips in clingfilm and reserve. Place the remainder in a saucepan with the sugar, orange flower water and water. Heat gently until the water boils, allow to boil for 1–2 minutes, then leave to cool.
2. Squeeze the juice from the lime.
3. Scoop out and discard the black seeds from the papaya, peel off the skin and cut the flesh into chunks.
4. Peel and slice the banana and toss in the lime juice.
5. Peel the skin from the lychees, cut them in half and remove the stones.
6. Mix together the papaya, banana, lychees, grapes, dates and kiwi fruit, pour over the cool syrup and divide between four serving dishes.
7. Mix the sauce ingredients together, transfer to a small bowl and scatter the reserved lime zest over the top.

Top: Blueberry Dream (*p 119*)
Bottom: Tropical Salad

TROPICAL FRAPPÉ

Serves 1
125 Calories per serving

To make a truly thirst quenching drink, chill the orange juice and buttermilk in the refrigerator before making this frappé.

juice of ½ a medium orange

½ medium mango

¼ pint (150ml) buttermilk, chilled

1 teaspoon clear honey

lime juice

slice of lime to garnish

1. Place the orange juice in a blender, scoop all the flesh from the skin of the mango and add to the orange juice with the buttermilk and honey. Process until smooth. Add lime juice to taste and process once again.
2. Pour the purée into a glass and decorate the side of the glass with a slice of lime.

Exchanges per serving: Fruit 1½
Milk ½
20 Optional
Calories

LOW-CALORIE LEMONADE

Serves 3
0 Calories per serving

If you are not keen on the flavour of mint, leave it out altogether or only use it to decorate the glass before serving.

2 lemons

artificial sweetener

1 pint (600ml) boiling water

few sprigs of mint

1. Peel the zest from both lemons and place with artificial sweetener equivalent to 7–8 tablespoons of sugar in a bowl. Pour over the boiling water, add a large sprig of mint and leave until completely cold.
2. Strain the water into a large jug. Squeeze the juice from the lemons and stir into the jug. Serve with ice cubes and decorate with fresh sprigs of mint. Makes just over 1 pint (600ml).

Exchanges per serving: Nil

FRUITY ICE CREAM SODA

Serves 4

50 Calories per serving

Chill the soda water well before completing this recipe.

1 medium orange

1 lemon

artificial sweetener

4fl oz (120ml) boiling water

½ pint (300ml) soda water, chilled

4oz (120g) vanilla ice cream

slices of orange and lemon

Exchanges per serving: Fruit ¼
50 Optional
Calories

1. Remove the zest from the orange and lemon with a potato peeler. Place the zest, and artificial sweetener equivalent to 3 tablespoons of sugar, in a bowl. Pour the boiling water into the bowl and leave until cold.
2. Strain the zest from the liquid, pour into a blender, add the chilled soda water and ice cream. Blend for 1 minute until very frothy.
3. Pour the ice cream soda into four glasses and decorate each glass with a slice of orange or lemon. Serve immediately.

VEGETARIAN VARIETIES

The vegetarian approach to cooking has been growing in popularity for several years, and you don't have to be a non-meat eater to enjoy the recipes in this section. The dishes we've chosen include eggs, cheese, milk, pulses, tofu and nuts which, with the exception of coconut and peanut butter, appear only in this section.

The versatility of lentils and beans is well-known – try our Eggs with Spicy Dhal Sauce (page 140) and Beany Cobbler (page 148). To prepare dried beans, soak them in cold water for several hours, drain them, cover with fresh cold water, bring to a rapid boil for 10–12 minutes and continue boiling until they're tender. Don't add salt to the water as it tends to toughen the skins.

Tofu, a bean curd, provides another important source of protein for vegetarians and non-vegetarians alike, and it contains practically no fat! It's available in different varieties: silken or soft tofu, smooth and easy to liquidise and great for 'cheesecakes'; firm tofu, which retains its shape and can be cubed and used to add texture and protein to a variety of dishes (both these varieties are bland and need to be marinated or cooked with other, strongly flavoured ingredients); and smoked tofu, which is also firm but distinctively smoky. These and other varieties are sold in packets and once opened, must be stored in the refrigerator and eaten within a few days.

Why not experiment with our meat-free dishes? You'll be delighted at how delicious they can be!

Celery Soup with Tofu (*p 128*

CELERY SOUP WITH TOFU

Serves 2

115 Calories per serving

Smoked tofu and celery make an interesting combination and the flavours complement each other wonderfully.

1 teaspoon margarine

1 small onion, chopped

10oz (300g) celery, sliced

1 tablespoon flour

½ teaspoon chervil or 2 teaspoons fresh chervil, chopped

½ pint (300ml) vegetable stock

¼ pint (150ml) skimmed milk

salt and pepper

squeeze of lemon juice

3oz (90g) smoked tofu

2 sprigs of chervil (optional)

1. Melt the margarine in a saucepan, add the onion and stir-fry for 3–4 minutes.
2. Stir the celery into the saucepan, sprinkle in the flour and stir well. Add the chervil and stock and bring to the boil, stirring all the time. Reduce the heat, cover the saucepan and simmer for 20–25 minutes.
3. Transfer the celery and stock, etc. to a blender or food processor and process until smooth.
4. Return the celery purée to the saucepan, stir in the milk and season to taste with salt, pepper and lemon juice.
5. Cut the smoked tofu into small cubes and add to the soup. Stir over a moderate heat, pour into warm soup bowls and garnish with the sprigs of chervil.

> **Exchanges per serving:** **Fat ½**
> **Milk ¼**
> **Protein ½**
> **Vegetable 2**
> **15 Optional**
> **Calories**

BEAN SOUP

Serves 2

135 Calories per serving

Make sure you rinse the canned kidney beans well before adding them to the recipe.

1 teaspoon vegetable oil

1 clove garlic, chopped

1 small onion, chopped

1 stick celery, chopped

2 teaspoons tomato purée

¼ teaspoon basil or 1 teaspoon chopped fresh basil

½ pint (300ml) vegetable stock

6oz (180g) drained canned red kidney beans

pinch of chilli powder

salt

2oz (60g) shelled broad beans

Exchanges per serving: Fat ½
Protein 1
Vegetable 1
5 Optional
Calories

1. Heat the oil in a saucepan, add the garlic and onion and stir-fry for 3 minutes. Add the celery and stir-fry for a further 2 minutes.
2. Stir the tomato purée, basil, stock, kidney beans, chilli powder and a little salt into the saucepan. Bring to the boil, stirring all the time. Reduce the heat, cover and simmer for 25 minutes.
3. Plunge the broad beans in boiling salted water for 4 minutes, drain and pop the beans out of their waxy skins.
4. Transfer the kidney bean mixture to a blender or food processor and process until smooth.
5. Pour the bean purée into a clean saucepan, add the broad beans, bring to the boil and simmer for 1–2 minutes. Pour into two warm soup bowls and serve.

LENTIL SOUP

Serves 2
170 Calories per serving

This is a simple soup to make and can be left to simmer while you prepare a snack or main meal to accompany it.

1 teaspoon vegetable oil

1 clove garlic, finely chopped

1 onion, chopped

½ teaspoon ground coriander

½ teaspoon ground cumin

3oz (90g) split red lentils

16fl oz (480ml) vegetable stock

salt and pepper

2 sprigs of fresh coriander

1. Heat the oil in a small saucepan and stir-fry the garlic and onion for 2–3 minutes.
2. Stir the spices into the saucepan and mix in the lentils and stock.
3. Bring to the boil, stirring occasionally. Reduce the heat, cover the saucepan and simmer for 15–20 minutes.
4. Pour the lentil mixture into a blender or food processor and process until smooth.
5. Return to a clean saucepan and adjust the seasoning, adding salt and pepper to taste. Pour into two warm bowls and garnish with the fresh coriander.

Exchanges per serving: Fat ½
Protein 1½
Vegetable ½

LENTIL PÂTÉ

Serves 4
105 Calories per serving

This pâté is delicious served with a light salad and warm strips of pitta bread or melba toast.

1 medium onion, finely chopped

3oz (90g) split red lentils

1 clove garlic, crushed

½ pint (300ml) water

3oz (90g) curd cheese

salt and pepper

1. Place the onion, lentils, garlic and water in a saucepan. Bring to the boil over a high heat and boil rapidly for 10 minutes. Reduce the heat to low and simmer, uncovered, for 20–25 minutes, stirring occasionally, until the mixture is reduced to a thick purée.
2. Leave the purée until cold, add the curd cheese and mix well. Season with salt and pepper.
3. Spoon the pâté into a small dish or individual small ramekins, cover and chill well before serving.

Exchanges per serving: Protein 1
Vegetable ¼
5 Optional
Calories

CRUNCHY RICE SALAD

Serves 2

355 Calories per serving

This salad can be stored in a plastic container and taken on a picnic, or eaten as a snack lunch at work. If you plan to take it on a long journey, leave out the watercress as it will wilt fairly quickly.

For the dressing:

2½ tablespoons low-fat natural yogurt

1 teaspoon olive oil

1 teaspoon lemon juice

salt and pepper

For the salad:

3oz (90g) long grain brown rice

salt

1 medium apple

1 teaspoon lemon juice

½ red pepper, seeded and chopped

2 tablespoons chopped spring onions

1oz (30g) raisins or sultanas

1½oz (45g) pecans or walnuts, roughly chopped

few sprigs of watercress

1. Whisk together the dressing ingredients and put to one side.
2. Boil the rice in salted water according to the packaging instructions until it's cooked and the water has been absorbed – about 30–40 minutes.
3. Stir the dressing and rice together; leave to cool.
4. Quarter and core the apple, chop and toss in the lemon juice.
5. Mix together the rice, apple, red pepper, spring onions, raisins and pecans. Stir well.
6. Spoon the salad into a serving dish and garnish with sprigs of watercress.

Exchanges per serving: Bread 1½
Fat 1¼
Fruit 1
Protein 1½
Vegetable ½
10 Optional
Calories

FRUITY BEETROOT SALAD

Serves 2

175 Calories per serving

Use freshly cooked beetroot for this salad, which is sold by most greengrocers. The beetroot available in vinegar will tend to spoil the flavour.

6oz (180g) cooked beetroot

1 stick celery, chopped

1 medium orange

1 medium apple

1 teaspoon lemon juice

For the topping:

2oz (60g) curd cheese

5 tablespoons low-fat natural yogurt

1 tablespoon chopped spring onions

½oz (15g) walnuts

Exchanges per serving: Fat ¼
Fruit 1
Milk ¼
Protein 1
Vegetable 1½

1. Remove the outer skin from the beetroot, cut into ½-inch (1.25-cm) cubes and mix with the celery.
2. Using a sharp knife, remove the skin, including all the white pith, from the orange and cut between the segments to remove the membranes. Cut each segment in half and stir into the beetroot.
3. Cut the apple into quarters, remove the core and cut the flesh into cubes. Toss in the lemon juice and add to the beetroot. Transfer the beetroot mixture to a deep serving dish no more than 6 inches (15cm) in diameter.
4. Mix together the curd cheese, yogurt and spring onions and spread over the top of the salad.
5. Roughly chop the walnuts and scatter over the topping.

COLESLAW

Serves 4

110 Calories per serving

I prefer to use spring onions when making a coleslaw, but if you prefer, use half a medium mild onion instead. A food processor makes shredding and grating the ingredients simple and speedy.

3oz (90g) white cabbage

3 tablespoons chopped spring onions

3oz (90g) carrots, finely grated

1 stick celery, finely sliced

1oz (30g) walnut pieces

1oz (30g) sultanas

1 medium apple, preferably red skinned

1 tablespoon lemon juice

For the dressing:

8 teaspoons low-calorie mayonnaise

¼ teaspoon caraway seeds

salt and pepper

few endive, chicory, radicchio or Chinese leaves or any combination

Exchanges per serving: Fat 1¼
Fruit ½
Protein ½
Vegetable 1

1. Finely shred the white cabbage. Mix together the cabbage, spring onions, carrots, celery, walnuts and sultanas.
2. Cut the apple into quarters, remove the core, then cut in thin slices across the width of the quarter. Toss the apple in the lemon juice, then stir into the salad.
3. Mix together the mayonnaise and caraway seeds and season with salt and pepper. Stir the dressing into the salad.
4. Arrange the endive or other leaves around the edge of a salad bowl or serving plate and spoon the coleslaw into the centre.

Fruit and Nut Salad

Serves 2

200 Calories per serving

Use a strong-flavoured blue-veined cheese for this recipe, which will contrast well with the orange and nuts, as well as the honey salad dressing.

2-oz (60-g) mixture of lettuce, endive, radicchio and chicory

1oz (30g) cashew nuts, broken or roughly chopped

1oz (30g) cheese, e.g. Gorgonzola or Mycella, cubed or crumbled

4 radishes, sliced

½ red or green pepper (or a mixture) seeded

2oz (60g) fennel, thinly sliced

1 medium orange

For the dressing:

1 teaspoon honey

1 teaspoon olive oil or sesame oil

1 teaspoon wine vinegar

salt and pepper

1. Tear the lettuce leaves into pieces and mix together with the cashew nuts, cheese and radishes in a salad bowl.
2. Cut the pepper into thin half-circle slices and stir with the fennel into the salad bowl.
3. Using a sharp knife, remove the zest and white pith from the orange, divide into segments and remove the membranes, catching any juice which drips during preparation. Stir the orange segments into the salad.
4. To make the dressing, pour the reserved orange juice into a small screw-top jar, add the honey, oil, vinegar and salt and pepper. Shake well to mix. Alternatively, whisk together in a small bowl.
5. Pour the dressing over the salad and toss well.

Exchanges per serving: Fat 1
Fruit ½
Protein 1½
Vegetable 1
10 Optional
Calories

STUFFED ONIONS

Serves 4

160 Calories per serving

Serve an onion per person as a delicious accompaniment to a main meal.

4 × 8-oz (240-g) Spanish onions

1oz (30g) walnuts or pecans, finely chopped

1oz (30g) fresh wholemeal breadcrumbs

2oz (60g) strong-flavoured hard cheese, grated

salt and pepper

1 teaspoon vegetable oil

> Exchanges per serving: **Bread ¼**
> **Fat ½**
> **Protein 1**
> **Vegetable 2½**

1. Peel the onions and cut a very thin slice from the root end. Plunge in boiling water and boil for about 30 minutes until just cooked.
2. Remove the onions from the water, allow to drain and cool a little. Using a small sharp knife and teaspoon, cut a thin slice from the top of each onion and remove a proportion of the inside, leaving sufficient flesh to maintain the shape.
3. Chop the scooped-out onion and mix with the nuts, breadcrumbs and cheese. Season with salt and pepper.
4. Spoon the stuffing back into each onion, pressing it down gently. Pile any remaining stuffing on top.
5. Lay a piece of foil on a baking sheet and brush with some of the oil. Place the onions on top and brush with the remaining oil.
6. Bake at Gas Mark 5, 190°C, 375°F for 25–30 minutes.

ITALIAN-STYLE PASTA

Serves 2

275 Calories per serving

This low-fat version of the traditional Italian basil and pine nut sauce tastes very good indeed.

3oz (90g) wholewheat pasta such as bows, spirals, spaghetti, etc.

salt

½oz (15g) pine kernels

1 teaspoon olive oil

1 very small clove garlic, crushed

12 basil leaves, finely chopped

1 teaspoon tomato purée

1oz (30g) Parmesan cheese, finely grated

Exchanges per serving: Bread 1½
Fat ¾
Protein 1
5 Optional
Calories

1. Plunge the pasta in plenty of boiling salted water and cook according to the packaging instructions – about 10–12 minutes.
2. Grind the pine kernels. With such a small quantity, I find it easiest to do this in a mouli grater.
3. Heat the oil in a small saucepan, add the garlic and ground pine kernels and stir over a gentle heat until the nuts have absorbed the oil. Do not allow to brown. Remove from the heat.
4. Drain the cooked pasta, blending 2 tablespoons of the cooking water with the basil and tomato purée.
5. Return the saucepan with the pine kernels to a low heat and add the drained pasta and tomato mixture. Stir well until thoroughly heated through. Stir in the Parmesan cheese and serve immediately.

CRUNCHY STIR-FRY

Serves 2

235 Calories per serving

Alter the combination of vegetables to suit what's available, but blanch vegetables such as swede, parsnips, etc. before adding to the stir-fry.

For the marinade:

2 teaspoons tomato purée

2 tablespoons soy sauce

2 tablespoons water

1 clove garlic, crushed

For the stir-fry:

6oz (180g) firm tofu

3oz (90g) baby corn

salt

3oz (90g) cauliflower florets

2oz (60g) carrots, cut in strips

2oz (60g) mangetout, top and tailed

1 small courgette, sliced

1 teaspoon vegetable oil

½ teaspoon fresh chopped ginger

1 small onion, chopped

½ red pepper, seeded and cut in strips

1oz (30g) mooli, chopped

2oz (60g) bean sprouts

1oz (30g) halved almonds

pepper

1. Place all the marinade ingredients in a screw-top jar and shake well, or place in a basin and whisk together.
2. Cut the tofu into 1-inch (2.5-cm) cubes, pour the marinade over the tofu and leave for at least 1 hour to absorb the flavour, stirring occasionally.
3. Boil the corn in salted water for 2 minutes, add the cauliflower and carrots and continue boiling for a further 2 minutes. Add the mangetout and courgette and cook for 2 more minutes. Drain.
4. Heat the oil in a pan, add the ginger and stir-fry for 1 minute. Add the onion and red pepper and continue to stir-fry for 3–4 minutes.
5. Mix the tofu, marinade, all the blanched vegetables and mooli into the pan and stir over a moderate heat for about 4 minutes.
6. Add the bean sprouts and almonds and continue stirring over a moderate heat until completely heated through. Season to taste and serve.

Exchanges per serving: Bread ½
Fat 1
Protein 2
Vegetable 2½
5 Optional
Calories

Top: Vegetarian Kebabs *(p 146)*
Bottom: Crunchy Stir-Fry

EGGS WITH SPICY DHAL SAUCE

Serves 2

265 Calories per serving

This dish can either be served as a main meal followed by a fruit dessert, or eaten with a crisp mixed salad as a midday or supper time snack.

For the sauce:

1 teaspoon vegetable oil

1 clove garlic, finely chopped

1 onion, chopped

½ green chilli, seeded and chopped

½ teaspoon ground coriander

½ teaspoon ground cumin

½ teaspoon turmeric

1½ teaspoons tomato purée

3oz (90g) split red lentils

8fl oz (240ml) vegetable stock

salt and pepper

2 eggs

few sprigs of fresh coriander

1. To prepare the spicy dhal sauce, heat the oil in a small saucepan, add the garlic, onion and chilli and stir-fry for 2–3 minutes.
2. Stir the spices, tomato purée, lentils and stock into the saucepan and bring to the boil, stirring occasionally. Reduce the heat, cover and simmer for 15–20 minutes.
3. When the sauce has been cooking for 10 minutes, plunge the eggs into a saucepan of simmering water and simmer for 10 minutes.
4. Remove the eggs from the hot water and plunge into cold water until they are cool enough to handle. Remove the shells and cut the eggs in half lengthways. Place flat side down on a warm serving plate.
5. Transfer the sauce to a blender or food processor and blend until smooth.
6. Return the sauce to a clean saucepan, reheat and adjust the seasoning to taste. Pour the hot sauce over the eggs, garnish with the sprigs of fresh coriander and serve immediately.

Exchanges per serving: Fat ½
Protein 2½
Vegetable ½
5 Optional
Calories

CHEESE AND WALNUT CROQUETTES

Serves 3

310 Calories per serving

These croquettes are simple to make and may be served with hot crisp vegetables or a variety of crisp salads.

3oz (90g) fresh wholemeal breadcrumbs

2 tablespoons chopped spring onions

2oz (60g) walnuts, finely chopped

2oz (60g) curd cheese

2oz (60g) cheese, finely grated

1 egg, lightly beaten

1 tablespoon chopped parsley

1 teaspoon vegetable oil

Exchanges per serving: Bread 1
Fat 1
Protein 2½
10 Optional
Calories

1. Mix together the breadcrumbs, spring onions and walnuts.
2. Beat the cheeses together and gradually stir in the breadcrumbs, spring onions and walnuts.
3. Add the egg and parsley and bind the mixture together.
4. Divide the mixture into six even-sized pieces and, using your hands, shape into croquettes.
5. Heat the oil in a small frying pan, add the croquettes and cook for 10–15 minutes, turning occasionally until golden brown and heated through.

SIMPLE SOUFFLÉ OMELETTE

Serves 1

470 Calories per serving

This basic soufflé omelette can be served on its own or filled with a variety of fillings. Two variations are given, but always remember to prepare the filling before making the omelette.

2 eggs, separated

salt

1½ teaspoons margarine

pepper

2oz (60g) Cheddar, Double Gloucester or any other hard cheese, finely grated

**Exchanges per serving: Fat 1½
Protein 4**

1. Whisk the egg whites with a pinch of salt until peaking.
2. Melt the margarine in a non-stick 7-inch (18-cm) frying pan over a low heat.
3. Whisk the egg yolks with a little pepper. Using a metal spoon, fold the egg yolks and cheese into the whisked egg whites.
4. Increase the heat under the frying pan, add the egg mixture and leave over a moderate heat for 1–2 minutes. Meanwhile, preheat the grill.
5. Ease the edge of the omelette from the frying pan using a palette knife. When the underside looks golden brown, transfer the pan to the grill for just under a minute until the top just begins to colour.
6. Fold the soufflé omelette in half, slide onto a warm serving plate and serve immediately.

Pepper-Filled Egg Omelette (*p 144*)

Variation 1

265 Calories per serving

PEPPER-FILLED EGG OMELETTE

For the filling:

½ teaspoon margarine

½ red pepper, seeded and chopped

1 tablespoon chopped spring onions

Exchanges per serving: **Fat 2**
Protein 2
Vegetable 1

1. Melt the ½ teaspoon of margarine in a 7-inch (18-cm) non-stick frying pan, add the red pepper and spring onions and stir-fry for 3–4 minutes. Remove the pepper and spring onions from the pan and keep warm.
2. Make the soufflé omelette as described in the basic recipe, adding 1½ teaspoons of margarine to the same frying pan and omitting the cheese.
3. Remove the omelette from the grill, sprinkle the pepper and onion over half the omelette and fold over the other half. Slide on to a warm plate and serve immediately.

Variation 2

415 Calories per serving

CREAMY SPINACH-FILLED SOUFFLÉ OMELETTE

For the filling:

4oz (120g) spinach

1 teaspoon chopped chives

1 tablespoon single cream

salt and pepper

freshly grated nutmeg

Exchanges per serving: **Fat 1½**
Protein 3
Vegetable 1
35 Optional
Calories

1. Wash the spinach, shake off the excess water and roughly chop. Place in a saucepan, cover and cook over a moderate heat for 3–4 minutes. Drain well, stir in the chives and cream and season to taste with salt, pepper and nutmeg. Put to one side and reheat while grilling the omelette.
2. Make the soufflé omelette as described in the basic recipe, but using only 1oz (30g) of Parmesan cheese.
3. Spoon the hot filling on the grilled soufflé omelette, slide on to a warm plate and serve immediately.

CHEESE AND MUSHROOM SOUFFLÉ

Serves 2

390 Calories per serving

Serve this soufflé immediately to take full advantage of its spectacular appearance. If you prefer a plain cheese soufflé, leave out the mushrooms and add 1oz (30g) grated Parmesan cheese with the Cheddar cheese, remembering to increase the Protein Exchange by a half.

4 teaspoons margarine

½ small onion or shallot, finely chopped

2oz (60g) mushrooms, chopped

½oz (15g) flour

¼ pint (150ml) skimmed milk

3 eggs, separated

2oz (60g) mature Cheddar cheese, grated

good pinch powdered mustard

salt and pepper

cream of tartar

> **Exchanges per serving: Bread ¼**
> **Fat 2**
> **Milk ¼**
> **Protein 2½**
> **Vegetable ½**

1. Use a little of the margarine to grease a deep soufflé dish, 6 inches (15cm) in diameter.
2. Melt the remaining margarine in a 2-pint (1-litre 200-ml) saucepan, add the onion and stir-fry for 2–3 minutes. Add the mushrooms and stir-fry for a further 2 minutes.
3. Sprinkle the flour into the saucepan and cook over a low heat for 1–2 minutes, stirring all the time.
4. Remove from the heat and gradually blend in the milk. Bring to the boil, stirring continuously, and boil for 1–2 minutes. Allow to cool a little.
5. Beat the egg yolks and cheese into the sauce. Season to taste with mustard, salt and pepper.
6. Whisk the egg whites with a pinch of cream of tartar until peaking. Using a tablespoon, lightly fold them into the mushroom and cheese sauce. Transfer the mixture to the soufflé dish and bake at Gas Mark 4, 180°C, 350°F for 35 minutes until golden brown, well risen and just set. Serve immediately.

VEGETARIAN KEBABS

Serves 2

155 Calories per serving

Smoked tofu has its own distinctive flavour, but if you wish to use firm tofu, cut it into squares and place in a slightly stronger-flavoured marinade for a minimum of an hour.

2 peppers, preferably a mixture of red, green and yellow

12oz (360g) smoked tofu

3oz (90g) mushrooms

8 bulbous spring onions

4 baby tomatoes, halved, or 8 cherry tomatoes

1 large clove garlic, crushed

2 tablespoons lemon juice

2 teaspoons vegetable oil

salt and pepper

endive, lettuce or chicory leaves

Exchanges per serving: Fat 1
Protein 2
Vegetable 2

1. Cut the peppers in half, remove the core and seeds and cut into 1-inch (2.5-cm) squares). Plunge in boiling water and boil for 4 minutes. Drain.
2. Cut the smoked tofu into 1-inch (2.5-cm) cubes.
3. Halve or quarter the mushrooms according to their size.
4. Thread the peppers, tofu, mushrooms, spring onions and tomatoes on eight small or four large skewers.
5. Place the garlic, lemon juice, oil and seasoning in a screw-top jar and shake well to mix, or place in a small basin and whisk together.
6. Lay the kebabs over a flameproof dish and place under a moderate grill, brushing every few minutes with the lemon juice and oil. Grill for 8–10 minutes. Serve garnished with endive, lettuce or chicory leaves.

VEGETARIAN GRATINÉE

Serves 2

240 Calories per serving

You can adapt this recipe to suit your appetite. If you are very hungry, add an extra tomato and increase the amount of beans, or add another egg, but remember to alter the Exchanges accordingly.

½ green pepper, seeded

½ red pepper, seeded

salt

1 teaspoon vegetable oil

1 small onion, chopped

3oz (90g) drained canned kidney or butter beans

2 tomatoes, peeled and chopped

¼ teaspoon dried oregano, or 1 teaspoon chopped fresh oregano

pepper

2 eggs

2 tablespoons grated Parmesan cheese

1. Cut the green and red pepper into ½-inch (1.25-cm) squares, plunge in boiling salted water and boil for 4 minutes. Drain.
2. Heat the oil, add the chopped onion and stir-fry for 3–4 minutes.
3. Stir the peppers, beans, tomatoes and oregano into the onions and mix well. Season with salt and pepper, cover the pan and leave over a low heat for 4–5 minutes.
4. Transfer the vegetable mixture to an au gratin dish, make two wells in the vegetables and break the eggs into the dips. Sprinkle the vegetables and eggs with the cheese.
5. Cook about 3 inches (7.5cm) away from a moderately hot grill for about 10 minutes, depending on how well you like your eggs cooked.

Exchanges per serving: Fat ½
Protein 1½
Vegetable 2
30 Optional
Calories

BEANY COBBLER

Serves 2

545 Calories per serving

This warming meal is ideal for a winter's evening. The base can be prepared in advance, then heated through and the scones baked on top.

7½oz (225g) drained canned mixed beans, e.g. kidney, butter, haricot

1 medium can chopped tomatoes (397g)

1 onion, chopped

6oz (180g) small cauliflower florets

4 tablespoons weak stock or water

½ teaspoon mixed herbs

For the cobbler scone topping:

4oz (120g) plain flour

1½ teaspoons baking powder

pinch of salt

pinch of powdered mustard

4 teaspoons margarine

1½oz (45g) mature Cheddar cheese, finely grated

4 tablespoons skimmed milk to mix, plus 1 teaspoon to glaze

> **Exchanges per serving: Bread 2**
> **Fat 2**
> **Protein 2**
> **Vegetable 3½**
> **10 Optional Calories**

1. Mix together the beans, tomatoes, onion, cauliflower, stock and herbs in an ovenproof casserole. Bring to the boil, reduce the heat, cover and simmer for 15 minutes.
2. While the vegetables are cooking, make the scone topping. Reserve 1 teaspoon flour. Sieve the remaining flour, baking powder, salt and mustard into a bowl.
3. Rub in the margarine, which, if possible, has been stored in the freezer, until the mixture resembles fresh breadcrumbs. Stir in the cheese.
4. Make a well in the centre of the flour, add the 4 tablespoons of milk and mix to form a soft dough with a round-bladed knife. If necessary, add a little extra milk.
5. Sprinkle the reserved flour over the work surface and rolling pin. Roll out the dough to a ½–¾-inch (1.25–2-cm) thickness. Either cut into six triangles or, using a 2-inch (5-cm) round cutter, cut into 6 scones. Leave to stand for about 10 minutes.
6. Arrange the scones on top of the vegetable mixture and brush each one with the remaining milk. Bake in a preheated oven, Gas Mark 7, 210°C, 425°F for about 15 minutes until golden.

Tofu and Bean Burgers

Serves 2

345 Calories per serving

Use firm, well-drained tofu for this recipe to make it easy to shape the mixture into burgers.

9oz (270g) firm tofu

6oz (180g) drained canned red kidney beans

1 teaspoon soy sauce

1 teaspoon tomato purée

½ teaspoon yeast extract

½ teaspoon mixed herbs

1 medium onion, grated

1 egg, lightly beaten

1oz (30g) fresh wholemeal breadcrumbs

salt and pepper

4 teaspoons wholemeal flour

1 tablespoon vegetable oil

1. Place the tofu, kidney beans, soy sauce, tomato purée and yeast extract in a blender or food processor and process until smooth.
2. Spoon the tofu mixture into a bowl and stir in the herbs, onion, egg and breadcrumbs. Season with a little salt and pepper. Cover and refrigerate for 2–3 hours or longer.
3. Sprinkle the work surface with flour. Divide the tofu mixture into four equal-sized portions and shape each one into a round burger about 1 inch (2.5cm) thick.
4. Brush a piece of foil with a little of the oil and lay on the rack of a grill pan. Transfer the tofu and bean burgers to the greased foil and brush with the remaining oil.
5. Cook under a moderately hot grill for 15–20 minutes, turning once.

Exchanges per serving: Bread ½
Fat 1½
Protein 3
Vegetable ½
20 Optional
Calories

TOFU HOT-POT

Serves 2
230 Calories per serving

This dish is a meal in itself. You can adjust the seasoning to suit your taste by adding more vinegar or soy sauce.

9oz (270g) firm tofu

1 tablespoon honey

8 teaspoons soy sauce

4 teaspoons tomato purée

2 tablespoons wine vinegar

2 tablespoons orange juice

1 tablespoon vegetable oil

1 clove garlic, finely chopped

½ teaspoon chopped fresh ginger

1 leek, cut in ½-inch (1.25-cm) slices

½ red pepper, seeded and cut in ½-inch (1.25-cm) squares

½ green pepper, seeded and cut in ½-inch (1.25-cm) squares

6-oz (180-g) mixture of swede, carrot and parsnip, cubed

3oz (90g) water chestnuts, sliced

4fl oz (120ml) vegetable stock

3oz (90g) drained canned beans, e.g. kidney, flageolet, haricot

1 teaspoon cornflour

2 teaspoons water

2oz (60g) beansprouts

salt and pepper

1. Cut the tofu into 1-inch (2.5-cm) squares.
2. Mix together the honey, soy sauce, tomato purée, vinegar and orange juice, pour over the tofu and leave to marinade for 1 hour, stirring occasionally.
3. Heat the vegetable oil, add the garlic, ginger, leek and peppers and stir-fry for 4 minutes.
4. Stir the swede, carrot, parsnip, water chestnuts, stock, beans and marinade into the stir-fry mixture, bring to the boil, reduce the heat, cover and simmer for 15 minutes, stirring from time to time.
5. Add the tofu to the saucepan and simmer for a further 4 minutes.
6. Mix the cornflour to a smooth paste with the water and add to the vegetables with the beansprouts. Boil for 1–2 minutes, stirring all the time. Adjust the seasoning and serve.

Exchanges per serving: Bread ½
Fat 1½
Protein 2
Vegetable 2½
50 Optional Calories

VEGETABLE CURRY

Serves 2

300 Calories per serving

Serve this hot curry with a bowl of brown rice and some plain low-fat natural yogurt. If you prefer a milder curry, reduce the amount of chilli and cayenne.

2 teaspoons vegetable oil

1 teaspoon finely chopped fresh ginger

1 clove garlic, finely chopped

1 chilli, seeded and finely chopped

½ teaspoon turmeric

1 teaspoon ground coriander

½ teaspoon ground cumin

½ teaspoon cayenne

2 leeks, thickly sliced

12oz (360g) mixed root vegetables such as swede, parsnip, carrot and turnip, cut in 1-inch (2.5-cm) cubes

3oz (90g) peas

9oz (270g) firm tofu, cut in 1-inch (2.5-cm) cubes

6oz (180g) drained canned chick peas or kidney beans

8fl oz (240ml) mixed vegetable juice

salt

approximately 1 teaspoon lemon juice

1. Heat the oil in a saucepan, add the ginger, garlic and chilli and stir-fry for 1–2 minutes. Remove from the heat.
2. Stir the turmeric, coriander, cumin and cayenne into the saucepan.
3. Add all the prepared vegetables, tofu and chick peas to the saucepan and stir in the mixed vegetable juice. Bring to the boil over a moderate heat, cover, reduce the heat and simmer for 30 minutes.
4. Remove the vegetable curry from the heat and season to taste with salt and lemon juice.

> **Exchanges per serving: Fat 1**
> **Fruit ½**
> **Protein 2½**
> **Vegetable 3½**

VEGETABLE MOUSSAKA

Serves 4

265 Calories per serving

I used plain firm tofu when testing this recipe, but the smoked tofu would be equally successful.

1lb (480g) aubergines

salt

9oz (270g) firm tofu

1 onion, chopped

12oz (360g) drained canned beans such as a mixture of flageolet, butter, and kidney beans

1 medium can chopped tomatoes (14oz/397g)

1 teaspoon oregano

2 eggs

4 tablespoons skimmed milk

2oz (60g) cheese, finely grated

Exchanges per serving: Protein 2¾
Vegetable 3
5 Optional
Calories

1. Cut the aubergines into ½-inch (1.25-cm) slices, place in a colander or sieve and sprinkle well with salt. Leave to drain for about 20 minutes, rinse well and drain.
2. Cut the tofu into 1-inch (2.5-cm) cubes, transfer to a saucepan and add the onion, beans, tomatoes and oregano. Bring to the boil, reduce the heat and simmer for 10 minutes.
3. Plunge the aubergine into boiling water and boil for 2–3 minutes. Drain.
4. Arrange half the aubergine over the base of a deep ovenproof dish, spoon the tofu and tomato mixture on top and cover with the remaining slices of aubergine.
5. Cover loosely and bake at Gas Mark 4, 180°C, 350°F for 25 minutes.
6. Beat the eggs and milk lightly together, stir in the cheese, pour over the aubergine and bake at the same temperature for a further 15 minutes.

VEGETABLE LASAGNE

Serves 4
485 Calories per serving

Use a deep dish for this recipe, and one that is able to hold three layers of whichever variety and shape of lasagne you choose.

½ teaspoon vegetable oil

For the vegetable sauce:

1 teaspoon vegetable oil

1 onion, chopped

1 stick celery, chopped

4oz (120g) carrots, diced

2oz (60g) okra, cut in 1-inch (2.5-cm) lengths

2 medium cans chopped tomatoes (2 × 14oz/397g)

1 teaspoon oregano

1 tablespoon chopped parsley

6 tablespoons water

1lb 2oz (540g) smoked tofu, cubed

3oz (90g) drained canned kidney beans

6oz (180g) wholewheat, verdi or plain lasagne

salt

For the cheese sauce:

1 tablespoon margarine

3 tablespoons flour

¼ teaspoon powdered mustard

½ pint (300ml) skimmed milk

3oz (90g) cheese, grated

1. Grease the lasagne dish with ½ teaspoon oil.
2. To make the vegetable sauce, heat the oil in a large saucepan, add the onion and stir-fry for 3–4 minutes. Add the celery, carrots, okra, canned tomatoes, herbs and water, stir well and bring to the boil. Cover, reduce the heat and simmer for 20–25 minutes.
3. Add the smoked tofu and kidney beans to the vegetable sauce. Keep warm.
4. Boil the lasagne in salted water according to the packaging instructions and drain well.
5. While the lasagne is cooking, make the cheese sauce. Melt the margarine in a saucepan, stir in the flour and remove from the heat. Add the mustard and gradually blend in the milk. Bring to the boil, stirring all the time, and boil for 2 minutes. Stir in about 2½oz (75g) of the cheese.
6. Spread a very thin layer of cheese sauce over the base of the lasagne dish and cover with pieces of lasagne. Spoon half the vegetable sauce over the lasagne and cover with a second layer of lasagne. Top with the remaining vegetable sauce and remaining lasagne and pour over the cheese sauce.
7. Sprinkle over the reserved cheese and bake at Gas Mark 4, 180°C, 350°F for 30–35 minutes.

Exchanges per serving:	Bread 1½
	Fat 1
	Milk ¼
	Protein 2½
	Vegetable 3½
	30 Optional Calories

RED FRUIT SALAD

Serves 2

90 Calories per serving

This combination of red fruit tastes delicious in the delicately flavoured rosewater syrup. If you don't have any rosewater, it is well worth buying a bottle from a chemist and experimenting by adding it to various fruit dishes.

For the syrup:

1 strip of lemon zest

juice of ½ a lemon

5 tablespoons water

1 tablespoon sugar

1 teaspoon rosewater

For the salad:

5-oz (150-g) mixture of raspberries and strawberries

5-oz (150-g) wedge water melon

1 large fig, sliced

2oz (60g) cherries

1 medium red dessert plum

Exchanges per serving: Fruit 2
30 Optional
Calories

1. Place the strip of lemon zest, lemon juice, water, sugar and rosewater in a saucepan and place over a low heat until the sugar has dissolved. Bring to the boil, cover the saucepan, remove from the heat and leave until cool. Remove and discard the strip of lemon zest.
2. Place the raspberries in the serving dish, halve the strawberries and mix in with the raspberries.
3. Remove the outer skin from the wedge of water melon and cut the flesh into cubes, removing the black seeds. Stir into the raspberries and strawberries with the fig.
4. Stone the cherries, cut in half or leave whole and add to the other fruit.
5. Cut the plum in half, remove the stone and cut the fruit into thin wedges. Mix into the other fruit.
6. Pour the cool syrup over the fruit and leave in the cool for at least an hour before serving.

STRAWBERRY WHIZZ

Serves 2

140 Calories per serving

This deliciously simple recipe is ideal for a hot summer's day.

1 medium banana

5oz (150g) strawberries

3oz (90g) firm tofu

2 teaspoons honey

½oz (15g) flaked almonds

Exchanges per serving: Fat ¼
Fruit 1½
Protein 1
20 Optional
Calories

1. Peel and roughly chop the banana; place in a blender or food processor.
2. Chop any large strawberries, crumble the tofu and add to the blender with the honey.
3. Process until smooth and transfer to two serving glasses.
4. Sprinkle the flaked almonds onto a baking sheet and grill for 1–2 minutes until light brown.
5. Scatter the toasted almonds over the strawberry and banana purée. Chill until ready to serve.

HONEYED PEARS

Serves 2

115 Calories per serving

This sweet dessert is delicious with low-fat natural yogurt.

4fl oz (120ml) apple juice

4 teaspoons clear honey

2-inch (5-cm) stick of cinnamon

2 medium pears

Exchanges per serving: Fruit 1½
40 Optional
Calories

1. Place the apple juice, honey and cinnamon in a saucepan and heat gently until the honey has dissolved.
2. Peel the pears, halve and scoop out the cores. Transfer immediately to the prepared syrup. Cover the saucepan and place over a very low heat for 10–15 minutes until the pears are just cooked.
3. Remove the pears from the syrup, increase the heat and boil fiercely for 2–3 minutes. Pour over the pears and leave to cool.
4. Discard the cinnamon stick before serving.

COATED FRUITS

Serves 4

245 Calories per serving

Vary this recipe to make use of seasonal fruit. Use blackberries instead of raspberries, and gooseberries or rhubarb instead of the apple and raspberries.

10oz (300g) raspberries

1 medium cooking apple, peeled, cored and sliced

2–3 tablespoons water

artificial sweetener

For the topping:

3 eggs

3 tablespoons sugar

½ pint (300ml) skimmed milk

2oz (60g) ground almonds

Exchanges per serving: Fat ½
Fruit ¾
Milk ¼
Protein 1¾
45 Optional Calories

1. Reserve a few raspberries for decoration and place the remainder in a saucepan with the apple and water. Cover the saucepan and place over a low heat for about 10 minutes, or until the fruit is cooked.
2. Transfer the fruit to a blender and process until smooth. Sweeten the fruit purée to taste with artificial sweetener and pour into a serving dish. Leave to cool, then transfer to the refrigerator.
3. Lightly whisk the eggs and sugar with a little milk. Heat the remaining milk until steaming and stir into the eggs. Strain the egg mixture back into the saucepan and stir continuously over a very low heat until the custard thickens. Do not allow to boil.
4. Remove the custard from the heat and stir in the ground almonds. Allow to cool, then spoon over the cold fruit purée. Leave until cold.
5. Before serving, decorate the top of the custard with the reserved raspberries.

RED BERRY SPECIAL

Serves 4

130 Calories per serving

This dessert can be made with a variety of berries. I chose a mixture of raspberries and strawberries, but tayberries, loganberries and blackberries may be used instead. You may need to adapt the amount of sugar to suit the different types of fruit.

15-oz (450-g) mixture of strawberries and raspberries

5 teaspoons cornflour

4 tablespoons caster sugar

4fl oz (120ml) red grape juice

5fl oz (150ml) low-fat natural yogurt

Exchanges per serving:	Fruit 1
	Milk ¼
	75 Optional Calories

1. Reserve a few raspberries for decoration. Place the remaining fruit in a blender or food processor and process until smooth. Sieve to remove the pips.
2. Blend the cornflour and sugar to a smooth paste with a little of the grape juice. Stir in the remaining grape juice and fruit purée.
3. Bring the fruit mixture to the boil, stirring all the time, and boil for 1 minute, stirring continuously.
4. Leave the mixture to cool, stirring occasionally. Mix in the yogurt and transfer to four serving dishes or glasses. Leave until cold, decorate with the reserved raspberries and serve.

FRUIT AND OATMEAL DESSERT

Serves 3
160 Calories per serving

The basic oatmeal and honey mixture may be used to make a wide range of different desserts. Experiment by adding it to different fresh or drained canned fruits.

½ pint (300ml) skimmed milk

2 tablespoons clear honey

1oz (30g) porridge oats

1oz (30g) raisins or sultanas

5 tablespoons low-fat natural yogurt

4 medium apricots, stoned and chopped

approximately 2 teaspoons lemon juice

3 lemon slices to garnish

Exchanges per serving:	Bread ¼
	Fruit 1
	Milk ½
	40 Optional Calories

1. Heat the milk until steaming, stir in the honey, porridge oats and raisins and bring to the boil, stirring all the time. Reduce the heat and simmer for 6–7 minutes, stirring continuously.
2. Remove the saucepan from the heat and leave until cold, stirring from time to time.
3. Stir the yogurt and apricots into the cold oatmeal mixture. Add lemon juice to taste and spoon into three serving glasses. Decorate each glass with a slice of lemon.

PEACH MERINGUE

Serves 2

215 Calories per serving

The firm peach, crisp meringue and deliciously soft stuffing make a wonderful combination.

2 medium peaches
finely grated zest of ½ a medium orange
1oz (30g) ground almonds
½ teaspoon honey
1 egg white
pinch of cream of tartar
3 tablespoons caster sugar

> **Exchanges per serving: Fat ½**
> **Fruit 1**
> **Protein 1**
> **105 Optional**
> **Calories**

1. Cut the peaches in half and remove the stones.
2. Using a teaspoon, scoop a little of the peach flesh out from around the cavity left by the stone, but don't use much force or the peaches will lose their shape. Chop the flesh.
3. Mix together the scooped out peach flesh, orange zest, ground almonds and honey. Spoon this stuffing back into each peach half.
4. Whisk the egg white with the cream of tartar until peaking, add half the sugar and whisk again until stiff. Fold in the remaining sugar.
5. Arrange the peach halves on an ovenproof plate or dish, pile the meringue on top of each half and bake in a preheated oven, Gas Mark 5, 190°C, 375°F, for 10 minutes. Allow to cool for a few minutes before serving.

Top: Fruit and Oatmeal Dessert (p 15
Bottom: Peach Meringues

NUTTY CHILLED CUSTARD

Serves 4

180 Calories per serving

This versatile recipe can be made with a coffee or vanilla-flavoured base, and topped with a variety of drained canned or fresh fruit.

½ teaspoon margarine

¾ pint (450ml) skimmed milk

2 eggs

2 tablespoons clear honey

1–1½ teaspoons instant coffee powder or ½ teaspoon vanilla essence

4oz (120g) drained canned apricots

For the topping:

5fl oz (150ml) low-fat natural yogurt

2 teaspoons clear honey

½oz (15g) flaked almonds, toasted

1. Grease a 1½-pint (900-ml) ovenproof dish with the margarine.
2. Heat the milk until steaming and remove from the heat.
3. Lightly whisk the eggs, honey and coffee or vanilla together. Whisk in the hot milk. Strain into the greased dish, place the dish in a baking tin half filled with hot water and bake at Gas Mark 3, 160°C, 325°F for about 50 minutes or until set. Leave until cold.
4. Chop the apricots and scatter evenly over the top of the cold custard.
5. Stir the yogurt and honey together and spread over the apricots. Scatter with the toasted almonds and serve.

Exchanges per serving: Fat ¼
Fruit ¼
Milk ½
Protein ¾
50 Optional
Calories

SPEEDY SNACKS

Whenever I hear the term 'fast food', I imagine people hurrying into takeaways for hamburgers and pizzas. These high-fat convenience foods don't fit in with the principles of a balanced, healthy diet, and in this chapter we show you how to prepare delicious, healthy food – fast!

All the recipes are quick and easy to make and, although not designed as main-meal dishes, many of them are ideal for lunch or supper – for instance Ham and Egg Bakes (page 179) and Prawn Salad (page 185).

Many people now own microwave ovens, which are useful for thawing and reheating food quickly, and some of our recipes have been devised with these in mind, for instance Stuffed Jacket Potatoes (page 163). All the recipes have been tested in a 650 watt microwave oven, but always follow the manufacturers' recommendations for your own particular oven, because cooking times are determined by the wattage of the oven, the temperature, shape and density of the food to be cooked and the amount of fat, sugar and moisture it contains. Allow microwaved food 'standing' time after cooking (this is when the cooking process is completed), use suitable containers and pierce all foods, like jacket potatoes, which are cooked in their skins. Remember, if you double the quantity of a microwave recipe, the cooking and standing times must be altered.

Why not try the recipes in this section? Not only are they simply healthy, they'll probably take you less time to prepare than it takes to walk round to the takeaway when you're in need of a fast and filling snack.

STUFFED ROLLS

Serves 2

245 Calories per serving

This recipe has been included with microwave owners in mind. Although the rolls can be cooked in a conventional oven, they take about 20–25 minutes longer.

2 × 1½-oz (45-g) wholemeal or granary rolls

1 egg, beaten

3oz (90g) cooked ham or corned beef, chopped

2 teaspoons tomato purée

3 tablespoons chopped spring onions

1 small clove garlic, crushed (optional)

1 tablespoon grated Parmesan cheese

dash of chilli sauce

salt

Exchanges per serving: Bread 1½
Protein 2
20 Optional
Calories

1. Cut a ½-inch (1.25-cm) slice from the top of each roll. Pull out the inside of the base of the roll, leaving the crust intact. Place the bread from inside the rolls into a blender and process to make breadcrumbs.
2. Mix together the egg, ham or corned beef, tomato purée, spring onions, garlic and cheese. Stir in the breadcrumbs and season well with chilli sauce and salt.
3. Spoon the stuffing back into the roll crusts and top with the reserved ½-inch (1.25-cm) slices. Cook, either by placing on a plate and cooking on full power in a microwave oven for 1 minute 45 seconds, leaving to stand for 2 minutes then serving, or wrap loosely in foil and bake at Gas Mark 6, 200°C, 400°F for 20–25 minutes until the egg has set and the filling is hot.

STUFFED JACKET POTATOES

Serves 1

285 Calories per serving

These recipes are mainly for microwave owners, but if you are using a conventional oven on a high temperature, it is possible to reheat the stuffed potatoes in 15–20 minutes.

6-oz (180-g) potato

For the filling:

1½oz (45g) cooked ham, chopped

1 tablespoon chopped spring onion

½oz (15g) mature Cheddar cheese, grated

2 tablespoons skimmed milk

salt and pepper

> **Exchanges per serving: Bread 2**
> **Protein 2**
> **10 Optional**
> **Calories**

1. Wash and dry the potato, pierce the skin all over, place on a sheet of kitchen paper and microwave on full power for 4 minutes 30 seconds. Remove from the oven, wrap in aluminium foil and leave to stand for 4 minutes.
2. Cut the potato in half and scoop out the middle, leaving the skins intact.
3. Mash the potato and mix in the ham, spring onion, cheese and milk. Season to taste with salt and pepper.
4. Spoon the filling back into the potato skins, place the two potato halves back in the microwave on a sheet of kitchen paper and microwave on full power for 1 minute 45 seconds. Leave to stand for 2 minutes before serving.

Variation: 1

235 Calories per serving

6-oz (180-g) potato

1 tablespoon cream cheese

2 teaspoons chopped chives

2oz (60g) peeled prawns

salt and pepper

> **Exchanges per serving: Bread 2**
> **Protein 2**
> **100 Optional**
> **Calories**

1. Cook the potato as previously described, cut in half and scoop out the middle, leaving the skins as shells.
2. Mash the potato, cream cheese and chives together. Stir in the prawns and season with salt and pepper.
3. Spoon the filling back into the potato skins, place on a sheet of kitchen paper and reheat on full power for 1 minute 45 seconds. Leave to stand for 2 minutes before serving.

Variation: 2

330 Calories per serving

6-oz (180-g) potato

1 tablespoon low-fat natural yogurt

4 teaspoons chopped spring onions

2oz (60g) corned beef, diced

1 tablespoon grated Parmesan cheese

salt

dash of pepper sauce

1. Cook the potato as previously described, cut in half and scoop out the middle, leaving the skins as shells.
2. Mash the potato, yogurt and spring onions together. Stir in the corned beef and Parmesan cheese. Season to taste with salt and pepper sauce.
3. Spoon the filling back into the potato skins, place on a sheet of kitchen paper and reheat on full power for 1 minute 45 seconds. Leave to stand for 2 minutes before serving.

Exchanges per serving: Bread 2
Protein 2
40 Optional
Calories

SAVOURY SCRAMBLE

Serves 2

205 Calories per serving

Microwave ovens make beautifully textured scrambled eggs, but, if you wish to use a conventional method, stir-fry the spring onions and mushrooms in a saucepan with the melted margarine for 2–3 minutes, then add the remaining ingredients and stir over a moderate heat until just set.

1½ teaspoons margarine

1 tablespoon chopped spring onions

2oz (60g) button mushrooms, sliced

3 eggs

3 tablespoons skimmed milk

2oz (60g) cottage cheese

salt and pepper

1. Place the margarine in a basin or jug and melt on full power for 50 seconds.
2. Add the spring onions and mushrooms and cook at full power for 1 minute 30 seconds.
3. Beat the eggs, milk, cottage cheese and seasoning into the container and return to the oven. Cook on full power for 2 minutes 30 seconds, removing and stirring well once or twice during this final cooking time.
4. Remove from the oven when just set, stir well and serve.

Exchanges per serving: Fat ¾
Protein 2
Vegetable ½
10 Optional
Calories

Selection of Stuffed Jacket Potatoes (*pp 163, 164*)

TOMATO FAN

Serves 1
190 Calories per serving

This attractive-looking snack makes a wonderfully light lunch or supper dish.

1 tomato

1 hard-boiled egg

2oz (60g) cottage cheese

2 teaspoons low-calorie mayonnaise

1 teaspoon lemon juice

1 tablespoon chopped spring onions

a few chicory , lettuce or endive leaves

Exchanges per serving: Fat 1
Protein 2
Vegetable 1½

1. Using a sharp knife, make several slices down through the tomato, almost to the base.
2. Thinly slice the hard-boiled egg into as many slices as the tomato. Place a slice of egg in between each slice of tomato.
3. Mix the cottage cheese, mayonnaise, lemon juice and spring onions together.
4. Arrange the salad leaves on a small serving plate and spoon the cottage cheese mixture in a circle in the centre. Flatten and spread the mixture evenly and place the tomato fan on top.

PITTA PARCELS

Serves 1

220 Calories per serving

Here are three different ways of filling pitta bread to make extremely quick snacks. Experiment with ideas of your own by using leftover salad ingredients and cold cooked meats, etc.

1 mini wholemeal pitta

1 tablespoon crunchy peanut butter

½oz (15g) raisins, roughly chopped

½ medium orange, divided into segments

½oz (15g) sprigs of watercress

Exchanges per serving: Bread 1
Fat 1
Fruit 1
Protein 1

1. Place the pitta under a hot grill for about 2 minutes, turning once until lightly crisp, or place on a sheet of kitchen paper and microwave on full power for 15 seconds. Put to one side while preparing the filling.
2. Mix the peanut butter and raisins together.
3. Slit along one side of the pitta and spread the peanut butter and raisin mixture inside.
4. Fill the 'pouch' with the orange segments and sprigs of watercress. Serve immediately.

Variation: 1
160 Calories per serving

1 mini wholemeal pitta

2 teaspoons low-calorie mayonnaise

1 teaspoon lemon juice

1oz (30g) beansprouts

1 teaspoon chopped chives

2oz (60g) peeled prawns

salt and pepper

1 lettuce leaf

1. Heat the pitta as previously described.
2. Mix the mayonnaise and lemon juice together, stir in the beansprouts, chives and prawns and season to taste with salt and pepper.
3. Slit along one side of the pitta. Lay the lettuce leaf inside and pile the prawn and mayonnaise filling on top. Serve immediately.

Exchanges per serving: Bread 1
Fat 1
Protein 2
Vegetable ½

Variation: 2
265 Calories per serving

1 mini wholemeal pitta

1 hard-boiled egg

1-oz (30-g) slice of tongue

few slices of cucumber

2–3 radicchio or lettuce leaves, shredded

1 black olive, stoned and quartered

salt and pepper

1 teaspoon low-fat spread

1. Heat the pitta as previously described.
2. Slice the hard-boiled egg and cut the tongue into strips. Mix the egg, tongue, cucumber, shredded leaves and olive together. Season with a little salt and pepper.
3. Slit along one side of the pitta. Spread the inside of the pitta with the low-fat spread, then spoon the filling into the pouch. Serve immediately.

Exchanges per serving: Bread 1
Fat ½
Protein 2
Vegetable ½
5 Optional
Calories

SAVOURY GRAPEFRUIT CUPS

Serves 2

180 Calories per serving

Choose a really crisp lettuce for this recipe so that the leaves stand up higher than the grapefruit and hold the filling. The red-tinged lettuce varieties always look very attractive.

1 medium grapefruit

a few crisp lettuce leaves

1 medium tomato

4oz (120g) smoked plain or peppered mackerel fillets, skinned and flaked

1 stick celery, chopped

2 black olives, stoned and sliced

For the dressing:

4 teaspoons low-calorie mayonnaise

2 teaspoons chopped chives

salt and pepper

> **Exchanges per serving: Fat 1**
> **Fruit 1**
> **Protein 2**
> **Vegetable 1**
> **5 Optional**
> **Calories**

1. Cut the grapefruit in half and using a grapefruit knife, remove the flesh. Cut between the membranes to remove the half segments of fruit, reserving any juice which runs out during preparation.
2. Line each grapefruit half with lettuce leaves, making sure that the leaves stand 1–2 inches (2.5–5cm) above the edge of the grapefruit.
3. Plunge the tomato into boiling water for 30 seconds and remove the skin. Cut the tomato into thin wedges.
4. Mix together the grapefruit, tomato, flaked mackerel, celery and black olives.
5. Mix the low-calorie mayonnaise, chives and any reserved grapefruit juice. Season with salt and pepper and stir the dressing into the salad.
6. Pile the salad into the grapefruit and lettuce cups and serve.

CROUSTADES

Serves 2

250 Calories per serving

These croustades make ideal snacks, especially when accompanied by a mug of piping hot soup or some fruit.

2 × ¾-oz (20-g) slices of crustless wholemeal bread

1½ teaspoons margarine

For a hot filling:

1 teaspoon vegetable oil

1 shallot or small onion, finely chopped

4½oz (135g) cooked or drained canned butter beans

1oz (30g) curd cheese

1oz (30g) Cheddar cheese, grated

salt

dash of pepper sauce

1. Flatten each slice of bread by rolling evenly and gently with a rolling pin. Spread each side of the bread thinly with the margarine.
2. Press the bread into two individual Yorkshire pudding tins. Bake at Gas Mark 6, 200°C, 400°F for 12–14 minutes.
3. While the croustades are cooking, prepare the hot filling. Heat the oil in a small saucepan, add the shallot or onion and stir-fry for 4–5 minutes.
4. Mash the butter beans and curd cheese together, stir into the stir-fried onion and stir over a low heat until heated through. Add the grated cheese and stir until melted.
5. Season the beany cheese filling with salt and a little pepper sauce. Spoon into the hot croustades and serve immediately.

Exchanges per serving: Bread ¾
Fat 1¼
Protein 1½
Vegetable ¼

Variation:

190 Calories per serving

2 × ¾-oz (20-g) slices of crustless wholemeal bread

1½ teaspoons margarine

For a cold filling:

4oz (120g) curd cheese

1oz (30g) Parma ham, chopped

2 tablespoons low-fat natural yogurt

1. Mix together the curd cheese, Parma ham, yogurt, chives, tomato purée and Parmesan cheese.
2. Season to taste with salt and pepper, then spoon into the cool croustades and garnish each with half a black olive.

1 tablespoon chopped chives

1 teaspoon tomato purée

2 teaspoons grated Parmesan cheese

salt and pepper

1 black olive, stoned and halved

Exchanges per serving: Bread ¾
Fat ¾
Protein 1½
25 Optional
Calories

TUNA TAGLIATELLE

Serves 2

350 Calories per serving

While the pasta is boiling, prepare and stir-fry the other ingredients so that when the tagliatelle is drained, the whole dish can be assembled quickly.

3oz (90g) tagliatelle, wholewheat or verdi

salt

1½ teaspoons vegetable oil

1 leek, thinly sliced

1 small clove garlic, finely chopped

1 red pepper, cored, seeded and cut in thin strips

1 tablespoon cream cheese

3 tablespoons skimmed milk

4oz (120g) drained canned tuna, flaked

pepper

1 tablespoon finely grated Parmesan cheese

2 lemon wedges

1. Cook the tagliatelle in boiling salted water according to the packaging instructions.
2. Heat the oil in a wok or saucepan, add the leek, garlic and red pepper and stir-fry for about 5 minutes.
3. Mix the cream cheese with a little of the milk in a small basin, gradually blend in the remaining milk and stir into the vegetables with the tuna. Season with salt and pepper.
4. Drain the pasta, add to the vegetables and mix together over a moderate heat for 1–2 minutes.
5. Transfer the tuna tagliatelle to a warm serving plate and sprinkle with the cheese. Serve with lemon wedges.

Exchanges per serving: Bread 1½
Fat ¾
Protein 2
Vegetable 1½
75 Optional
Calories

SPAGHETTI ALLA CARBONARA

Serves 3

350 Calories per serving

This is particularly good with wholewheat or verdi spaghetti, or even a mixture of the two.

4½oz (135g) spaghetti
salt
1½ teaspoons olive oil
1 onion, chopped
2 eggs
3 tablespoons single cream
2oz (60g) cooked ham, chopped
pepper
1oz (30g) Parmesan cheese, grated
2 teaspoons chopped parsley

Exchanges per serving: Bread 1½
Fat ½
Protein 1½
Vegetable ¼
40 Optional
Calories

1. Boil the spaghetti in salted water according to the packaging instructions for about 12 minutes.
2. Heat the oil in a wok or saucepan, add the onion and stir-fry for 4–5 minutes until soft. Remove from the heat.
3. Beat together the eggs and cream, stir in the ham, season with a little salt and plenty of pepper and mix in the cheese.
4. Drain the spaghetti and place the wok or saucepan containing the onion over a moderate heat.
5. Add the spaghetti and egg mixture to the onion and stir to mix. Remove from the heat and stir until the egg thickens. The heat from the spaghetti should be sufficient to do this but, if necessary, return to a low heat. Sprinkle with the parsley and serve.

STUFFED EGGS

Serves 2

150 Calories per serving

While the eggs are boiling, why not prepare a mixed salad to go with the completed recipe?

2 eggs

2oz (60g) white crabmeat

1 tablespoon low-calorie mayonnaise

1 tablespoon low-fat natural yogurt

1½ teaspoons chopped chives

salt and pepper

paprika

Exchanges per serving: Fat ¾
Protein 2
5 Optional
Calories

1. Place the eggs in a small saucepan, cover with cold water and bring to the boil. Boil for 10 minutes, plunge into cold water and remove the shells.
2. Cut the eggs in half lengthways. Using a teaspoon, scoop out the egg yolks and place in a small bowl.
3. Mash the egg yolks, crabmeat, mayonnaise and yogurt and chives together. Season well with salt and pepper.
4. Spoon the egg yolk mixture back into the white halves, dust with a little paprika and serve.

Variation

185 Calories per serving

2 eggs

2oz (60g) liver sausage

1 tablespoon chopped spring onions

1 teaspoon capers, rinsed and chopped

2 tablespoons low-fat natural yogurt

salt and pepper

4 small sprigs of parsley

Exchanges per serving: Protein 2
10 Optional
Calories

1. Prepare the eggs as previously described, scoop out the yolks and place in a small bowl.
2. Mash the egg yolks, liver sausage, spring onions, capers and yogurt together. Season well with salt and pepper.
3. Spoon the egg yolk mixture back into the white halves and garnish with the sprigs of parsley.

PEANUT SPIRALS

Serves 2

290 Calories per serving

The crunchy peanut butter sauce gives an unusual texture and flavour to the pasta, but use smooth peanut butter if you would prefer a smoother sauce.

3oz (90g) wholewheat or multicoloured pasta spirals

salt

1 teaspoon olive oil

1 small onion or shallot, chopped

½ red pepper, seeded and chopped

1½oz (45g) button mushrooms, sliced

2 tablespoons crunchy peanut butter

4 tablespoons skimmed milk

> **Exchanges per serving: Bread 1½**
> **Fat 1½**
> **Protein 1**
> **Vegetable 1**
> **10 Optional**
> **Calories**

1. Boil the pasta in salted water according to the packaging instructions – about 10–12 minutes.
2. While the pasta is cooking, heat the oil in a small saucepan, add the onion and red pepper and stir-fry for 4–5 minutes until just soft.
3. Add the mushrooms to the saucepan, stir round for about 1 minute, then remove from the heat.
4. Blend the peanut butter and milk together.
5. Drain the pasta. Return the onion, pepper and mushroom mixture to the heat and stir in the pasta and peanut butter sauce. Stir over a low heat until thoroughly heated through.

FRANKFURTER SUPPER

Serves 2

355 Calories per serving

A wok is ideal for cooking the frankfurter mixture, but if you don't own one, use a saucepan and stir frequently to prevent the ingredients sticking to the base of the pan.

3oz (90g) quick-boil rice or pasta

salt

1½ teaspoons vegetable oil

1 onion, chopped

½ green pepper, seeded and cut in half circles

2oz (60g) button mushrooms, sliced

1 tomato, peeled and chopped

good pinch of powdered mustard

4oz (120g) frankfurters, cut into 1-inch (2.5-cm) lengths

5 tablespoons low-fat natural yogurt

Exchanges per serving: Bread 1½
                           Fat ¾
                           Milk ¼
                           Protein 2
                           Vegetable 1¼

1. Cook the rice or pasta in salted water according to the packaging instructions.
2. Heat the oil in a wok or saucepan, add the onion and pepper and stir-fry for 4–5 minutes.
3. Add the mushrooms, tomato, mustard and frankfurters to the onion and pepper and stir well. Cover the wok and leave over a moderate heat for about 4 minutes, stirring from time to time.
4. Remove the frankfurter mixture from the heat and stir in the yogurt.
5. Drain the rice or pasta and serve with the frankfurters.

TOASTED SANDWICHES

Serves 1

320 Calories per serving

You probably already have the ingredients used for these toasted sandwiches. If you own an electric toaster, you may prefer to use that instead of the grill.

2 × 1-oz (30-g) slices wholemeal bread

1½ teaspoons margarine

1 tablespoon peanut butter, smooth or crunchy

½ medium banana, sliced

sprinkling of lemon juice

Exchanges per serving: Bread 2
Fat 2½
Fruit 1
Protein 1

1. Spread the margarine on one side of each slice of the bread. The margarine-spread sides will form the outside of the sandwich.
2. Turn the slices of bread over and spread half the peanut butter on each slice.
3. Arrange the slices of banana on one layer of peanut butter, sprinkle with a little lemon juice and top with the other slice of bread so that the peanut butter side touches the banana.
4. Place under a preheated grill until golden brown and crisp. Turn and grill the under side.

Variation: 1

250 Calories per serving

2 × 1-oz (30-g) slices wholemeal bread

1½ teaspoons margarine

2oz (60g) drained canned tuna, flaked

dash of lemon juice

½ teaspoon chopped chives

salt and pepper

few slices of cucumber

Exchanges per serving: Bread 2
Fat 1½
Protein 2

1. Mash the tuna and season to taste with lemon juice, chives, salt and pepper.
2. Spread the filling over the two dry sides of bread, lay the cucumber over the tuna and sandwich the cucumber between the tuna.
3. Cook as above.

Variation: 2
320 Calories per serving

2 × 1-oz (30-g) slices wholemeal bread

1½ teaspoons margarine

1oz (30g) drained canned salmon, flaked

2oz (60g) curd or cottage cheese

dash of chilli sauce

salt

1 tomato, sliced

1. Mix together the salmon and cheese. Season to taste with the chilli sauce and salt.
2. Spread the cheese and salmon mixture over both dry sides of bread, lay the tomato slices over one slice and top with the other slice of bread spread with the cheese and salmon mixture.
3. Cook as above.

Exchanges per serving: Bread 2
Fat 1½
Protein 2
Vegetable 1

HAM AND EGG BAKES

Serves 2

180 Calories per serving

Serve this recipe with salad and a warm crusty roll or piece of French bread which can be wrapped in foil and heated in the oven while the eggs are cooking.

½ teaspoon margarine

2oz (60g) cooked ham, chopped

2 teaspoons chopped chives

2 eggs

2 tablespoons single cream

1. Use the margarine to grease two individual ramekins.
2. Place half the ham in each ramekin, sprinkle 1 teaspoon chives into each and make a slight dip in the centre.
3. Break the eggs into each dip, pour over the cream and transfer the ramekins to a baking tin half filled with hot water. Bake at Gas Mark 4, 180°C, 350°F for about 15 minutes until set.

Exchanges per serving: Fat ¼
Protein 2
35 Optional
Calories

Variation:
Use 2oz (60g) peeled prawns in place of the cooked ham.

BROCCOLI AND CAULIFLOWER SPECIAL

Serves 2

435 Calories per serving

This recipe can be made with either broccoli or cauliflower on their own or, as suggested below, a mixture of the two. It's possible now to buy broccoli and cauliflower together in the same pack in some supermarkets.

9oz (270g) cauliflower florets

6oz (180g) calabrese broccoli, stalks roughly chopped

salt

For the sauce:

1 tablespoon margarine

3 tablespoons flour

¼ teaspoon powdered mustard

½ pint (300ml) skimmed milk

3oz (90g) mature Cheddar cheese, grated

½oz (15g) fresh breadcrumbs

2 tomatoes

6 anchovy fillets

4 black olives, stoned and halved

1. Cook the cauliflower and broccoli for about 12 minutes in boiling salted water until just cooked but still a little crisp.
2. While the vegetables are cooking, make the sauce. Melt the margarine in a saucepan, stir in the flour and remove from the heat. Add the mustard and gradually blend in the milk. Bring to the boil, stirring all the time, and boil for 2 minutes. Remove from the heat and stir in about 2½oz (75g) of the cheese.
3. Drain the cauliflower and broccoli and arrange in an ovenproof dish. Pour over the sauce and sprinkle with the breadcrumbs and reserved cheese. Place under a moderate grill until beginning to brown.
4. Slice the tomatoes and cut the anchovies in half lengthways. Remove the dish from the grill, arrange the tomatoes around the edge of the dish and the anchovies and olives decoratively on top. Return to the grill for a further 2–3 minutes.

> **Exchanges per serving: Bread ¼**
> **Fat 1½**
> **Milk ½**
> **Protein 1½**
> **Vegetable 3**
> **70 Optional Calories**

SALMON TOASTS

Serves 2

310 Calories per serving

This basic recipe can be used to suit whatever is in your storecupboard. Instead of the sweetcorn you can use other drained canned vegetables, and the salmon can be replaced with tuna. However, remember to alter the Exchanges accordingly.

2 teaspoons margarine

5 teaspoons flour

¼ pint (150ml) skimmed milk

1 tablespoon chopped chives or spring onions

4oz (120g) drained canned salmon, flaked

3oz (90g) drained canned sweetcorn

lemon juice

salt and pepper

2 × 1-oz (30-g) slices of bread

1 teaspoon low-fat spread

1. Heat the margarine in a saucepan, stir in the flour and remove from the heat. Gradually blend in the milk.
2. Bring the sauce to the boil, stirring all the time, and boil for 1–2 minutes. Stir in the chives, salmon and sweetcorn and season to taste with lemon juice, salt and pepper.
3. Toast the slices of bread and reheat the salmon and sweetcorn sauce, stirring continuously.
4. Spread the toast with the low-fat spread and top with the salmon and sweetcorn. Serve immediately.

Exchanges per serving: Bread 1½
Fat 1¼
Milk ¼
Protein 2
25 Optional
Calories

BREAD-BASED PIZZAS

Serves 2

210 Calories per serving

This simple bread-based pizza tastes very good on wholemeal bread. For a change, leave out the mushrooms and add a few chopped red or green peppers.

1 teaspoon vegetable oil

½ clove garlic, finely chopped

1 shallot or small onion, finely chopped

1oz (30g) mushrooms, sliced

2 × 1-oz (30-g) slices bread, toasted

1 tomato, peeled and sliced

2oz (60g) Mozzarella cheese, thinly sliced

3 anchovy fillets, sliced lengthways

2 black olives, stoned and quartered

1. Heat the vegetable oil in a small frying pan, add the garlic and onion and stir-fry for 3–4 minutes. Add the mushrooms and stir-fry for a further 2 minutes.
2. Divide the stir-fried vegetables between the two slices of toast.
3. Arrange the slices of tomato on top of the onion and mushrooms. Cover with the sliced Mozzarella and arrange the anchovy fillets in a criss-cross pattern. Garnish with the black olives.
4. Cook under a hot grill until the Mozzarella is bubbling.

Exchanges per serving: Bread 1
Fat ½
Protein 1
Vegetable ¾
15 Optional
Calories

TACOS

Serves 2

265 Calories per serving

This recipe is ideal for microwave owners but, if your conventional oven is already in use, it can be made reasonably quickly – it's not worth heating the oven specially for the 4 minutes or so it takes to warm the taco shells.

1½ teaspoons vegetable oil

½ clove garlic, finely chopped

1 small onion, finely chopped

6oz (180g) cooked or drained canned kidney beans

1 tablespoon tomato purée

1 tablespoon water

2 taco shells

1oz (30g) Cheddar cheese, grated

a few lettuce leaves, shredded

4 teaspoons soured cream

Exchanges per serving: Bread 1
Fat ¾
Protein 1½
Vegetable ¼
30 Optional
Calories

1. Heat the oil in a small saucepan and stir-fry the garlic and onion for 4 minutes.
2. Add the kidney beans, tomato purée and water and mash well. Stir over a moderate heat until heated through.
3. Place the taco shells on a sheet of kitchen paper and microwave on full power for 30 seconds. Leave to stand while completing the filling.
4. Add the grated cheese to the bean mixture and stir over a very low heat until melted.
5. Divide the lettuce between the two shells, spoon the bean mixture on top of the lettuce and spoon the soured cream on top of the beans. Serve immediately.

PRAWN SALAD

Serves 2

210 Calories per serving

Quick-boil rice is a valuable storecupboard staple. It can be cooked in 3–5 minutes and, when it's cool, can be added to a variety of dishes like this prawn salad. The ready-prepared undressed salads available at supermarkets and delicatessens are also useful when you are short of time.

1½oz (45g) quick-boil long grain rice

4 teaspoons low-calorie mayonnaise

1 teaspoon lemon juice

½ teaspoon tomato purée

4oz (120g) peeled prawns

1oz (30g) sultanas

3-oz (90-g) mixture of lamb's lettuce, radicchio, endive, chicory, etc.

1 teaspoon chopped chives

Exchanges per serving: Bread ¾
Fat 1
Fruit ½
Protein 2
Vegetable ½
5 Optional
Calories

1. Cook the rice according to the packaging instructions, drain and spread out on a plate to cool.
2. Mix together the mayonnaise, lemon juice and tomato purée. Stir in the prawns and mix well.
3. Stir the sultanas into the cool rice.
4. Arrange the lettuce, etc. on two plates, pile the rice and sultanas in the middle and top with the prawn mixture. Sprinkle with the chopped chives.

CHEESY LEEKS

Serves 2
185 Calories per serving

Serve this simple recipe with a vegetable like grilled tomatoes, and crusty bread or toast.

9oz (270g) leeks, chopped

2 tablespoons water

salt

3oz (90g) curd cheese

1½oz (45g) mature Cheddar cheese, grated

pepper

lemon juice

> **Exchanges per serving: Protein 1½**
> **Vegetable 1½**

1. Place the chopped leeks in a saucepan, add the water and a pinch of salt and cover the saucepan. Place over a moderate heat and cook for 10–12 minutes until the leeks are tender.
2. Transfer the leeks and their cooking liquid to a blender, add the curd cheese and process until smooth.
3. Spoon the leek purée back into the saucepan, stir in the grated cheese and season to taste with salt, pepper and lemon juice. Stir over a low heat until the cheese has melted. Serve immediately.

WELSH RAREBIT

Serves 1
320 Calories per serving

This traditional snack is extremely quick to make. You can turn it into the more substantial Buck Rarebit, by topping with a poached egg.

2oz (60g) Cheddar cheese, grated

2 teaspoons brown ale

¼ teaspoon English mustard

½ teaspoon margarine

1-oz (30-g) slice bread

pepper

> **Exchanges per serving: Bread 1**
> **Fat ½**
> **Protein 2**
> **5 Optional**
> **Calories**

1. Place the cheese, brown ale, mustard and margarine in a saucepan and stir over a low heat until creamy. Allow to cool and thicken slightly.
2. Meanwhile, toast the bread.
3. Season the cheese mixture with a little pepper and spoon over the toast.
4. Lay the toast on a sheet of foil on the grill rack to prevent any cheese which may bubble off the bread from dripping into the grill pan.
5. Cook the rarebit under a very hot grill until golden brown and bubbling. Serve immediately.

CELEBRATION COOKING

S pecial-occasion cooking needn't be rich and fattening. Your guests are far more likely to appreciate attractively presented and flavoursome food, served in a relaxed, friendly atmosphere, and the recipes in this section will help you to provide just that.

Choose your ingredients carefully and allow time to prepare and garnish the dish imaginatively. Serve dressings and sauces separately so that guests can take as much or as little as they please. If your budget allows, entertaining provides the perfect excuse for serving the more expensive treats like salmon and fillet steak – see Seafarer's Favourite (page 194) and Beef Marsala (page 208) – but it's by no means essential to spend a lot of money. Make use of seasonal ingredients for impressive dishes like Individual Spinach Soufflés (page 193), and serve masses of crisp, piping hot vegetables or colourful salads to accompany main dishes. Always warm your serving plates so that as little heat as possible is lost from the food, and garnish with sprigs of fresh herbs and lightly cooked vegetables.

The recipes in this section are designed to make your lunch or dinner parties very special indeed.

SMOKED SALMON CHEESECAKE

Serves 4 or 6
245 Calories per serving
or 165 Calories per serving

This unusual starter serves six people if served whole or cut in individual wedges and placed on a bed of endive. Alternatively, it makes a delicious lunch when served with a variety of salads.

6 water biscuits

2 tablespoons margarine

5fl oz (150ml) low-fat natural yogurt

6oz (180g) curd cheese

1 teaspoon tomato purée

2 teaspoons chopped chives

2oz (60g) smoked salmon, chopped

2 tablespoons hot water

2 teaspoons gelatine

1 egg white

pinch of cream of tartar

1-inch (2.5-cm) wedge cucumber, sliced

few slices of lemon

1. Crush the water biscuits into crumbs, either by placing them in a plastic bag and pressing with a rolling pin, or by processing in a blender.
2. Melt the margarine, stir in the biscuit crumbs and 1 tablespoon of yogurt and mix well. Press the biscuit mixture onto the base of a loose-bottomed 6-inch (15-cm) cake tin.
3. Beat together the curd cheese, tomato purée, chives and smoked salmon, gradually adding the remaining yogurt.
4. Place the water in a small cup or basin, sprinkle in the gelatine and stand in a saucepan of simmering water until dissolved. Stir into the cheese and smoked salmon mixture.
5. Whisk the egg white with a pinch of cream of tartar. Using a metal tablespoon, fold the egg white into the cheese mixture. Spoon onto the biscuit base and chill until set.
6. To serve, slide a spatula or palette knife under the biscuit base and slide the cheesecake on to a plate. Decorate with slices of cucumber and lemon.

Exchanges per serving for 4:
Bread ¾
Fat 1½
Milk ¼
Protein 1¼
5 Optional Calories

Exchanges per serving for 6:
Bread ½
Fat 1
Protein ¾
25 Optional Calories

Canapés (p 190)

CANAPÉS

Serves 2
190 Calories per serving
(see also variations 1 and 2)

*It's easy to multiply this recipe when you're entertaining a large number of people,
which is when canapés are usually served. The same base can be filled with any one of
the three variations shown here. Allow three canapés per person, and use the leftover
bread trimmings to make fresh breadcrumbs.*

For the base:

**2oz (60g) thin sliced crustless bread, cut
into six decorative shapes**

4oz (120g) curd cheese

4 teaspoons low-fat natural yogurt

2 teaspoons chopped chives

For the topping:

2oz (60g) smoked salmon, thinly sliced

squeeze of lemon juice

lemon slices

sprigs of parsley

> **Exchanges per serving: Bread 1**
> **Protein 2**
> **10 Optional**
> **Calories**

1. Lightly toast each piece of bread and leave until cold.
2. Mix together the curd cheese and yogurt; spoon about three quarters of the mixture into a piping bag fitted with a small star nozzle.
3. Spread the remaining cheese mixture over the six toasted shapes and sprinkle with the chives.
4. Cut the smoked salmon into six pieces the same size as the toast, using the same cutter if necessary. Place all the trimmings from the salmon on top of the chives and cover with the salmon shapes.
5. Pipe the curd cheese mixture decoratively around the edge, or in a pattern on top of the salmon.
6. Sprinkle each canapé with a little lemon juice and decorate with small pieces of lemon slices and tiny sprigs of parsley.

Variation 1
245 Calories per serving

For the topping:

2oz (60g) liver sausage, thinly sliced

3 black olives, stoned and cut in wedges

> **Exchanges per serving: Bread 1**
> **Protein 2**
> **25 Optional**
> **Calories**

Follow the same method, using liver sausage
instead of the smoked salmon, and garnish with
black olives, lemon and parsley.

Variation 2
240 Calories per serving

For the topping:

2oz (60g) tongue, thinly sliced

½ kiwi fruit, thinly sliced and cut in halves or quarters

Follow the same basic method, using tongue instead of the smoked salmon, and garnish with kiwi fruit.

> **Exchanges per serving: Bread 1**
> **Protein 2**
> **35 Optional**
> **Calories**

STUFFED MUSHROOMS

Serves 4
130 Calories per serving

This delicious starter combines mushrooms, broad beans and prawns. Make sure you drain the mushrooms well.

1lb 6oz (660g) shelled fresh or frozen broad beans

salt

1 tablespoon lemon juice

4oz (120g) peeled prawns

2 tablespoons single cream

2 teaspoons chopped chives

pepper

good pinch freshly grated nutmeg

4 × 3-oz (90-g) field or open mushrooms

4 lettuce or endive leaves

1. Boil the broad beans in salted water for about 10 minutes, reserve 2–3 tablespoons of the cooking water, drain the beans and transfer to a blender or food processor.
2. Add 2 tablespoons of the reserved water to the beans and process until smooth, adding a little extra water if necessary. Sieve the purée to remove the waxy skins and add the lemon juice.
3. Reserve 1oz (30g) prawns for decoration, chop the remainder and stir into the sieved purée with the cream, chives and seasonings.
4. Remove the stalks from the mushrooms and put to one side to use in a soup or casserole, etc. Plunge the mushrooms in boiling water and boil for 2–3 minutes; drain well.
5. While the mushrooms are cooking, reheat the bean and prawn mixture.
6. Arrange each mushroom on a lettuce or endive leaf, top with the broad bean and prawn mixture and decorate with the reserved prawns. Serve immediately.

> **Exchanges per serving: Protein 1**
> **Vegetable 3**
> **20 Optional**
> **Calories**

STAR STARTER

Serves 4

105 Calories per serving

The dishes are surrounded by five or six endive leaves which make an attractive star shape. The salad can be prepared in advance, but don't add the dressing until ready to serve.

2 heads of endive, about 3oz (90g) each

5oz (150g) smoked mackerel fillet

2oz (60g) cucumber

1 medium orange

2 tablespoons chopped spring onions

For the dressing:

1 teaspoon olive oil

1 tablespoon lemon juice

¼ teaspoon Dijon mustard

salt and pepper

> **Exchanges per serving: Fat ¼**
> **Fruit ¼**
> **Protein 1¼**
> **Vegetable ¾**

1. Separate the endive leaves and arrange five or six leaves around the edge of each serving dish or bowl. Roughly chop the remaining leaves.
2. Flake the mackerel and place in a bowl with the chopped endive.
3. Cut the cucumber in ¼-inch (5-mm) slices and cut each slice in quarters.
4. Using a sharp knife, remove the peel and white pith from the orange and divide into segments, removing as much membrane as possible and catching any juices which run out during preparation.
5. Stir the orange and spring onions into the smoked mackerel mixture. Mix well, then spoon into the serving dishes.
6. Place the reserved orange juice and all the dressing ingredients into a screw-top jar and shake well to mix. Alternatively, whisk the ingredients in a small basin. Spoon over each salad and serve.

INDIVIDUAL SPINACH SOUFFLÉS

Serves 4

185 Calories per serving

Make sure all your guests are sitting at the table before removing the soufflés from the oven. The guests have to wait for the soufflés – the soufflés won't wait for the guests!

8oz (240g) fresh spinach

1 onion, finely chopped

4 teaspoons margarine

½oz (15g) flour

¼ pint (150ml) skimmed milk

3 eggs, separated

2 tablespoons finely grated Parmesan cheese

salt and pepper

good pinch freshly grated nutmeg

pinch of cream of tartar

Exchanges per serving: Fat 1
Protein ¾
Vegetable 1
40 Optional Calories

1. Wash the spinach well in several changes of water, chop roughly and place in a saucepan with the onion. Cover the saucepan and cook over a gentle heat for about 5 minutes. There should be sufficient water clinging to the spinach leaves to cook them but, if necessary, add a little extra. Drain well.
2. Melt the margarine in a small saucepan. Brush four individual ramekins with a little margarine and place on a baking sheet.
3. Return the margarine in the saucepan back to the heat, stir in the flour and mix well. Remove from the heat and gradually blend in the milk. Bring the sauce to the boil, stirring all the time, and boil for 1–2 minutes.
4. Stir the spinach and onion, the egg yolks, cheese, salt and pepper and nutmeg into the sauce. Adjust the seasoning to taste.
5. Whisk the egg whites and cream of tartar until peaking. Using a metal tablespoon, lightly fold them into the spinach sauce. Spoon the mixture into the greased ramekins and bake at Gas Mark 4, 180°C, 350°F for 25–30 minutes until well risen, golden brown on top and just set. Serve immediately.

SEAFARER'S FAVOURITE

Serves 4

320 Calories per serving

This unusual sauce made with leeks and watercress complements the rich flavour of salmon. Take care not to overcook the salmon steaks — the poaching time will vary according to the thickness of the fish.

For the sauce:

2 teaspoons margarine

6oz (180g) leeks, thinly sliced

2oz (60g) watercress, roughly chopped

4 tablespoons water

2 tablespoons single cream

2 teaspoons lemon juice

salt and pepper

For the salmon:

4 × 5-oz (150-g) salmon steaks or cutlets

4 tablespoons white wine

6 tablespoons water

lemon slices or wedges

sprigs of watercress

Exchanges per serving: **Fat ½**
Protein 4
Vegetable ¾
30 Optional
Calories

1. Melt the margarine in a wok or saucepan, add the leeks and stir-fry for about 4 minutes. Add the watercress and stir over a moderate heat for 1–2 minutes. Add the water, cover and simmer for 15 minutes.
2. Transfer the mixture to a blender or food processor, add the single cream and lemon juice and process until smooth.
3. Lay the salmon in a frying pan large enough to hold all the steaks, add the wine and water, cover and simmer over a very low heat for 8–10 minutes. Remove the salmon with a fish slice, transfer to a warm plate and keep warm in a low oven.
4. Increase the heat under the salmon cooking liquid and boil fiercely until reduced to about 4 tablespoons of liquid.
5. Mix the leek and watercress purée with the reduced cooking liquid. Reheat the sauce over a moderate heat, stirring continuously. Season with salt and pepper.
6. Serve the salmon garnished with the lemon slices or wedges and sprigs of watercress. The sauce should be served separately.

SMOKED WHITING FLAN

Serves 6

255 Calories per serving

This tasty flan makes an ideal lunch or supper dish accompanied by a variety of salads. Don't add salt to the filling – smoked fish is already salty.

For the flan:

5oz (150g) wholemeal or plain flour

pinch of salt

4 tablespoons margarine

approximately 2 tablespoons cold water

1 tablespoon wholemeal or plain flour

For the filling:

1 red pepper

10oz (300g) skinned, smoked whiting fillets

¼ pint (150ml) skimmed milk

small strip of lemon zest

2oz (60g) curd cheese

2 tablespoons chopped spring onions

2 eggs

pepper

> **Exchanges per serving: Bread ¾**
> **Fat 2**
> **Protein 2**
> **Vegetable ¼**
> **25 Optional Calories**

1. First of all, make the pastry. Stir the flour and salt into a bowl. Rub the margarine into the flour until the mixture resembles fresh breadcrumbs.
2. Gradually add the cold water and mix to form a dough with a round-bladed knife. If time allows, cover with clingfilm and refrigerate for 30 minutes.
3. Sprinkle the rolling pin and sheet of non-stick baking parchment with the remaining flour. Roll out the pastry and line a 7-inch (18-cm) flan ring with the pastry, gently pressing it down the sides.
4. Trim the top edge. Lay a piece of baking parchment in the flan, weigh down with a few dried beans or rice and bake at Gas Mark 6, 200°C, 400°F for 10 minutes. Remove the baking parchment and beans and bake for a further 4–5 minutes. Remove from the oven.
5. Place the red pepper under a hot grill, turning occasionally until black and blistering all over. Plunge in cold water, peel off the skin, remove the seeds and core and chop the pepper.
6. Place the smoked whiting, milk and lemon zest in a saucepan, cover and simmer for 5–7 minutes until the fish is cooked. Discard the lemon zest. Remove and flake the fish.
7. Beat together the curd cheese, red pepper and spring onions. Lightly beat the eggs and mix into the curd cheese with the flaked fish and milk. Season to taste with a little pepper.
8. Transfer the filling into the cooked flan case and return to the oven at Gas Mark 4, 180°C, 350°F for 25–30 minutes.

SOLE VÉRONIQUE

Serves 4

210 Calories per serving

Although it may seem fiddly, it is well worth removing the skins from the grapes – the result is a wonderful smooth texture.

3oz (90g) green grapes

4 × 4-oz (120-g) sole fillets, black skin removed

½ small onion, finely chopped

sprig of parsley

1 bay leaf

6 tablespoons white wine

4 tablespoons water

For the sauce:

1 tablespoon margarine

2 tablespoons flour

4fl oz (120ml) skimmed milk

3 tablespoons single cream

lemon juice

salt and pepper

1 teaspoon finely chopped parsley

Exchanges per serving: Fat ¾
Fruit ¼
Protein 3½
75 Optional
Calories

1. Plunge the grapes in boiling water. It is difficult to estimate how long the grapes should be in the water as varieties vary considerably, so remove a few with a slotted spoon after 1 minute and test to see if the skins will peel off. If not, boil for a little longer. Cut the peeled grapes in half and remove any pips.
2. Lay the sole fillets in a frying pan or large-based saucepan. Add the onion, parsley, bay leaf, white wine and water. Heat until simmering, cover the pan and leave to simmer for 5 minutes or until the sole is cooked.
3. Use a fish slice to remove the sole and transfer to a warm serving dish. Cover and keep warm in a low oven while making the sauce.
4. Boil the white wine mixture rapidly until reduced to 6 tablespoons of liquid. Strain.
5. Melt the margarine and stir in the flour. Remove the saucepan from the heat and gradually blend in the strained wine and water, milk and cream. Bring to the boil, stirring all the time. Add lemon juice, salt and pepper to taste. Add the halved grapes and stir over a low heat for 1 minute.
6. Pour the sauce over the sole, sprinkle with parsley and serve.

ROLLED TROUT FILLETS

Serves 4

240 Calories per serving

Trout fillets are now readily available in supermarkets. They make a delicious meal and can be prepared in advance, then cooked when required.

4 × 4½-oz (135-g) trout fillets

For the stuffing:

2 teaspoons margarine

6 tablespoons chopped spring onions

3oz (90g) watercress, chopped

3oz (90g) mushrooms, finely chopped

3oz (90g) fresh breadcrumbs

salt and pepper

1 teaspoon lemon juice

½ teaspoon margarine

lemon wedges or slices, and sprigs of watercress to garnish

Exchanges per serving: **Bread ¾**
Fat ½
Protein 3½
Vegetable ¾
5 Optional Calories

1. Remove the skin from the trout fillets. Lay the fish skin-side down and hold the tail of one fillet, cut under the flesh at the tail-end and, using a sawing motion, gradually work up the fish. Repeat with each fillet.
2. To make the stuffing, melt the 2 teaspoons of margarine in a saucepan, add the spring onions and stir-fry for 2 minutes. Add the watercress and mushrooms and stir-fry for a further 3 minutes. Mix in the breadcrumbs and season well with salt and pepper.
3. Lay the fillets flat with the sides which were covered by the skin facing up. Sprinkle with the lemon juice.
4. Divide the stuffing into four, lay the stuffing on the centre of each fillet, roll the fish up and secure with cocktail sticks.
5. Grease a large piece of foil with the remaining margarine, put the rolled trout fillets on the foil and fold the foil over to seal. Bake in a preheated oven, Gas Mark 5, 190°C, 375°F for 20 minutes.
6. To serve, remove the cocktail sticks and garnish the fillets with lemon wedges or slices, and sprigs of watercress.

STUFFED TOMATOES

Serves 2

255 Calories per serving

These fish-stuffed tomatoes can be served with a crisp mixed salad or a selection of hot vegetables. The cheese can be any hard cheese under 120 Calories per 1oz (30g), but I prefer a mature Cheddar.

1¼ teaspoons margarine

2 × 10–11-oz (300–330-g) tomatoes

salt

6oz (180g) smoked haddock fillet

½ small onion, chopped

1½oz (45g) fresh wholemeal or white breadcrumbs

½ teaspoon basil

1oz (30g) cheese, grated

pepper

Exchanges per serving: Bread ¾
Fat ½
Protein 3
Vegetable 3½
5 Optional Calories

1. Grease an ovenproof dish, just large enough to hold the tomatoes, with ¼ teaspoon margarine.
2. Cut a thin slice from each tomato, scoop out the pulp and chop. Sprinkle the inside of the tomatoes with salt and leave upside down to drain while preparing the filling.
3. Place the smoked haddock in a saucepan, cover with cold water and simmer very gently for about 10 minutes. Drain the fish, flake the flesh and discard the skin.
4. Melt the remaining margarine in a small saucepan, add the onion and stir-fry for 3–4 minutes. Add the chopped tomato pulp and continue stirring over a moderate heat for about 15 minutes until reduced to a thick pulp. If necessary, turn the heat up to boil off the liquid.
5. Stir the fresh breadcrumbs, basil and cheese into the onion and tomato mixture. Season with pepper and a little salt if necessary.
6. Rinse the tomato cases well with cold water. Drain. Divide the stuffing between them, place the slices of tomato on top and transfer to the greased dish. Cover loosely with foil and bake at Gas Mark 4, 180°C, 350°F for 30–40 minutes until heated through.

REFRESHING GRAPEFRUIT

Serves 4

85 Calories per serving

If you're short of time simply cut the grapefruit in half, but the decorative 'vandyked' edge makes the dish look very attractive.

2 medium grapefruit

3oz (90g) black grapes

½ avocado

For the dressing:

½ teaspoon clear honey

2 teaspoons chopped chives

2 teaspoons lemon juice

> **Exchanges per serving: Fruit 1¼**
> **55 Optional**
> **Calories**

1. Cut a series of 'v' shapes around the middle of each grapefruit, pull the halves apart and, using a grapefruit knife, remove the flesh. Catch any juice which escapes during preparation.
2. Divide the grapefruit segments and remove as much of the membrane as possible.
3. Cut the grapes in half and remove any pips.
4. Cut the avocado into pieces and toss in the grapefruit juice which was caught while the fruit was prepared. Remove the avocado with a slotted spoon.
5. Stir the avocado, grapefruit and grapes together; spoon back into the grapefruit halves.
6. Mix the honey, chives, lemon juice and any remaining grapefruit juice together, spoon over the fruit and serve.

CHICKEN IN WINE

Serves 2

250 Calories per serving

This simple recipe is made on the hob. All it needs is a green vegetable and plain boiled or saffron rice and you have a filling main course for a dinner party.

2 teaspoons vegetable oil

2 × 5-oz (150-g) skinned chicken breasts on the bone

1 clove garlic, finely chopped

1 onion, sliced

½ red pepper, seeded and cut in strips

2oz (60g) mushrooms, sliced

½ teaspoon tarragon

4fl oz (120ml) white wine

1 tablespoon cornflour

6 tablespoons chicken stock

salt and pepper

Exchanges per serving: Fat 1
Protein 3½
Vegetable 1
65 Optional
Calories

1. Heat 1 teaspoon of oil in a flameproof casserole or saucepan and turn the chicken breasts in the hot oil until they lose their pink colour. Remove and put to one side.
2. Heat the remaining oil, add the garlic and onion and stir-fry for 3–4 minutes. Add the pepper and mushrooms and stir-fry for a further 1–2 minutes.
3. Stir the tarragon and wine into the casserole. Blend the cornflour with the chicken stock and stir into the vegetables. Bring to the boil, stirring all the time. Add salt and pepper to taste.
4. Reduce the heat, return the chicken to the casserole, cover and leave over a low heat for 25–30 minutes until the chicken is cooked.

MANGO CHICKEN CASSEROLE

Serves 4

275 Calories per serving

Serve this casserole with saffron rice or jacket potatoes and a crisp green vegetable such as mangetout or French beans.

1 tablespoon margarine

4 × 6-oz (180-g) chicken breasts, skinned but still on the bone

2 large leeks, sliced

1 tablespoon flour

14fl oz (420ml) chicken stock

strip of lemon zest

½ medium mango, cubed

4 teaspoons cornflour

4 tablespoons single cream

1 tablespoon chopped parsley

Exchanges per serving: Fat ¾
Fruit ¼
Protein 4
Vegetable 1
50 Optional Calories

1. Heat 2 teaspoons of margarine in a flameproof casserole. Fry two pieces of chicken at a time for about 4 minutes, turning once, until they have lost their pinkness. Transfer to a plate.
2. Melt the remaining margarine in the casserole, add the leeks and stir-fry for 2–3 minutes. Sprinkle in the flour and gradually blend in the stock. Bring to the boil, stirring all the time.
3. Stir the strip of lemon zest and mango into the stock, add the chicken breasts and any juices which have run from them, cover and place in a preheated oven, Gas Mark 4, 180°C, 350°F for 1 hour.
4. Remove the chicken and arrange on a serving plate. Keep warm while completing the sauce.
5. Blend the cornflour with a little of the stock, pour back into the casserole and stir over a moderate heat. Boil for 1–2 minutes, stirring continuously.
6. Remove the lemon zest and stir in the cream. Pour the sauce over the chicken and sprinkle with the parsley.

CRANBERRY AND TURKEY CASSEROLE

Serves 4

235 Calories per serving

Serve this casserole with brown rice to absorb the fruit-flavoured gravy which the turkey fillets are cooked in.

2 teaspoons vegetable oil

1 clove garlic, finely chopped

4 × 4½-oz (135-g) skinned turkey breast fillets

2 leeks, thinly sliced

3oz (90g) baby corns, whole or halved

4fl oz (120ml) orange juice

6fl oz (180ml) chicken stock

4 teaspoons brown sugar

1 tablespoon cornflour

5oz (150g) cranberries

salt and pepper

2 teaspoons chopped parsley

1. Heat the oil in a flameproof casserole. Add the garlic and fry 2 pieces of turkey at a time for 4 minutes, turning once. Remove from the casserole.
2. Add the leeks, corn and orange juice to the casserole.
3. Blend the stock with the sugar and cornflour and stir into the casserole. Bring to the boil over a moderate heat, stirring all the time.
4. Add the cranberries and turkey to the casserole, season with a little salt and pepper and transfer to a preheated oven, Gas Mark 4, 180°C, 350°F for 35–40 minutes.
5. Remove from the oven, adjust the seasoning and sprinkle with the chopped parsley.

Exchanges per serving: Bread ¼
Fat ½
Fruit ½
Protein 3½
Vegetable ¾
30 Optional
Calories

PORK WITH BROCCOLI

Serves 2

285 Calories per serving

Remember to grill the pork before cutting it into strips. As fillet has so little fat, it doesn't lose quite as much weight as other cuts.

6oz (180g) calabrese broccoli

2 teaspoons vegetable oil

1 clove garlic, finely chopped

1 teaspoon finely chopped fresh ginger root

½ red pepper, seeded and cut into strips

½ small onion, chopped

9oz (270g) pork fillet or tenderloin, cut into 3 × ½-inch (1.25-cm) strips

3oz (90g) small button mushrooms, halved

2 teaspoons flour

4fl oz (120ml) vegetable stock

salt and pepper

1. Thinly slice the broccoli stalk and divide the head into small florets.
2. Heat the oil in a wok or saucepan, add the garlic, ginger, red pepper and onion and stir-fry for 3–4 minutes.
3. Add the pork, broccoli and mushrooms, sprinkle in the flour and gradually pour in the stock, stirring all the time. Add salt and pepper to taste.
4. Bring to the boil, stirring continuously. Reduce the heat, cover and simmer for 8–10 minutes.

Exchanges per serving: Fat 1
Protein 3½
Vegetable 2
10 Optional
Calories

PEPPERCORN PORK

Serves 4

260 Calories per serving

This is a delicious recipe, especially suited to a summer barbecue. However, it's just as good cooked under the grill!

4 teaspoons green peppercorns

¼ pint (150ml) cider

2 teaspoons vegetable oil

4 × 5-oz (150-g) boneless pork loin chops

2 tablespoons single cream

salt

Exchanges per serving: Fat ½
Protein 4
30 Optional
Calories

1. Rinse the peppercorns well and crush using a pestle and mortar, or place in a small basin and crush with the end of a rolling pin.
2. Stir the peppercorns, cider and oil together.
3. Lay the pork in a non-metallic container, pour over the cider marinade and leave in the cool for about 2 hours.
4. Transfer the pork to a barbecue grill or the rack of a grill pan and cook over hot coals or under a high heat for about 8–10 minutes or until cooked, turning once.
5. Bring the cider and peppercorn marinade to the boil in a small saucepan. Boil rapidly until reduced by about half. Remove from the heat, stir in the cream and season with a little salt.
6. Serve the chops on a warm serving plate with the peppercorn sauce poured evenly over each chop.

PORK STIR-FRY

Serves 4

315 Calories per serving

A wok is ideal for this recipe, but if you don't have one, use a saucepan – a frying pan may not be large enough.

1lb 4oz (600g) pork fillet

2 teaspoons vegetable oil

1 teaspoon chopped fresh ginger

1 onion, chopped

3oz (90g) carrot, cut in thin strips

3oz (90g) small courgettes, sliced

3 tomatoes, peeled and chopped

3oz (90g) dwarf beans, cut in 1-inch (2.5-cm) lengths

3oz (90g) drained canned sweetcorn

3oz (90g) beansprouts

2 tablespoons sherry

3 tablespoons single cream

salt and pepper

Exchanges per serving: Bread ¼
Fat ½
Protein 4
Vegetable 2
35 Optional Calories

1. Lay the pork fillet on a rack under a hot grill and cook, turning once, until the fat stops dripping. Allow to cool then cut into thin strips.
2. Heat the oil in a wok or saucepan. Add the ginger and onion and stir-fry for 4–5 minutes.
3. Add the carrot, courgettes, tomatoes, beans, sweetcorn and pork and stir-fry for 3–4 minutes. Cover the wok or saucepan and leave over a moderate heat for 5 minutes, stirring occasionally.
4. Stir in the beansprouts and sherry, increase the heat and boil rapidly for 1–2 minutes.
5. Stir in the cream, season with salt and pepper and serve.

BEEF MARSALA

Serves 4

315 Calories per serving

Many years ago I devised this recipe when some friends came to dinner. I don't usually make a note of recipes as I tend to make them up according to the occasion or availability of ingredients, but I made a brief note of this one. Kiwi fruit acts as a meat tenderiser, so don't cut out the marinade time.

4 × 4½-oz (135-g) rump or fillet steaks

3 kiwi fruit

2 teaspoons margarine

1 small onion, finely chopped

½ chilli, seeded and finely chopped

4fl oz (120ml) Marsala

3 tablespoons single cream

salt and pepper

Exchanges per serving: Fat ½
Fruit ¾
Protein 3½
Vegetable ¼
60 Optional
Calories

1. Wipe the steaks and pierce a few times with a fork.
2. Peel and mash two kiwi fruit. Spread the purée on both sides of each steak, place in a non-metallic container, cover and leave in the cool to marinate for 3–4 hours.
3. Melt the margarine in a saucepan, add the onion and chilli and stir-fry for 4–5 minutes. Put to one side until you're ready to grill the steak.
4. Remove the steak from the marinade, leaving any purée which sticks onto the steak. Transfer to a rack under a moderate grill and cook for 5–6 minutes, turning once, or until the fat has stopped dripping from the meat.
5. Stir the remaining marinade into the onion and chilli, add the Marsala and bring to the boil. Boil for 1–2 minutes, stir in the cream and season to taste with salt and pepper.
6. Peel the remaining kiwi fruit and slice thinly. Place two slices on top of each steak, pour over the Marsala sauce and serve.

CARPET BAG STEAK

Serves 4

290 Calories per serving

This is a variation of a traditional Australian recipe where fresh oysters are sewn into the steak. I rather like the flavour of the smoked oysters, and I'm sure your guests will enjoy it too! Don't pre-cook the steak before assembling this recipe.

1lb 4oz (600g) rump or fillet steak, 2 inches (5cm) thick

2 tablespoons lemon juice

1 tablespoon vegetable oil

salt and pepper

2½oz (75g) drained canned smoked oysters

4 tomatoes

1 teaspoon chopped basil

sprigs of watercress

Exchanges per serving: Fat ¾
Protein 4½
Vegetable 1

1. Cut horizontally through the steak to about 1 inch (2.5cm) from the edge so the steak opens like a bag, held at the sides and back edge.
2. Mix together the lemon juice, oil and a sprinkling of salt and pepper, pour over the steak, cover and leave to marinate for 1½–2 hours.
3. Drain the steak and reserve the marinade.
4. Arrange the oysters in the steak and use a thin piece of string to sew up the cut edge of the steak to completely hide the oysters.
5. Transfer the steak to the rack of a grill pan and place under a moderate heat for 5 minutes; turn and cook for a further 5 minutes. Brush the steak with the marinade and continue grilling for 15–20 minutes.
6. When the steak has been cooking for about 15 minutes, cut the tomatoes in half, sprinkle with the basil and place under the grill for the steak's last few minutes.
7. Transfer the steak to a serving plate, remove the string and garnish with the tomatoes and sprigs of watercress.

VEAL MEDLEY

Serves 4

225 Calories per serving

If you are unable to buy fresh baby corns, either use frozen ones and cook them in the same way, or use drained canned baby corns, which you don't have to boil first.

3oz (90g) baby corns

salt

14oz (420g) veal cut from the top rump

1 tablespoon vegetable oil

2 medium leeks, thinly sliced

4oz (120g) mushrooms, sliced

6 tablespoons single cream

2 teaspoons lemon juice

pepper

1 teaspoon finely chopped parsley

1. Boil the corn in salted water for 6–7 minutes; drain and cut into 1-inch (2.5-cm) pieces.
2. Lay the whole piece of veal on a rack under a moderate grill for 6–7 minutes, turning once. Thinly slice the veal and put to one side.
3. Heat the oil in a saucepan, add the leeks and stir-fry for 4 minutes. Add the mushrooms and veal and stir-fry for a further 4–5 minutes.
4. Add the corn and cream to the saucepan and continue stirring over a moderate heat until heated through. Season to taste with the lemon juice, salt and pepper and simmer for 1–2 minutes.
5. Transfer the veal, vegetables and sauce to a warm serving dish, sprinkle with parsley and serve immediately.

Exchanges per serving: Bread ¼
Fat ¾
Protein 3
Vegetable 1
50 Optional
Calories

WELLINGTON LAMB

Serves 4

295 Calories per serving

This dish can be prepared in advance as far as stage three – but it's advisable to reheat the dish and add the kiwi fruit for the last 5 minutes, otherwise it overcooks and collapses.

1lb 2oz (540g) lamb leg fillet

2 teaspoons vegetable oil

2 leeks, thinly sliced

1 red pepper, cored, seeded and cut into strips

6fl oz (180ml) vegetable stock

3oz (90g) button mushrooms, sliced

2 teaspoons clear honey

2 teaspoons soy sauce

1 tablespoon cornflour

2 kiwi fruit, sliced

salt and pepper

1. Lay the lamb fillet on a rack under a hot grill and cook, turning once, until the fat stops dripping. Allow to cool then slice thinly.
2. Heat the oil in a wok or saucepan, add the leeks and red pepper and stir-fry for 5 minutes.
3. Stir in the lamb, stock and mushrooms, cover and simmer for 15 minutes.
4. Blend the honey, soy sauce and cornflour together, stir into the lamb mixture and bring to the boil, stirring all the time. Reduce the heat and simmer uncovered for 10 minutes, stirring occasionally.
5. Add the slices of kiwi fruit and continue to simmer for a further 5 minutes. Adjust the seasoning and serve piping hot.

Exchanges per serving: **Fat ½**
Fruit ½
Protein 3½
Vegetable 1
20 Optional Calories

INDIVIDUAL FRUIT FONDUES

Serves 4

160 Calories per serving

This is a wonderfully easy dessert to serve at a dinner party. The dip can be prepared in advance and just stirred well before serving, and all the fruit, except the apricots, can be arranged and covered with clingfilm before the guests arrive.

1 tablespoon cocoa

2 tablespoons soft brown sugar

¼ teaspoon instant coffee powder

1oz (30g) cornflour

12fl oz (360ml) skimmed milk

3 tablespoons rum

4oz (120g) fresh pineapple

5oz (150g) strawberries

2 kiwi fruit

2 medium apricots

Exchanges per serving: **Bread ¼**
Fruit 1
Milk ¼
80 Optional Calories

1. Place the cocoa, sugar, coffee and cornflour in a small basin and blend to a smooth paste with a little milk.
2. Heat the remaining milk until steaming, pour in the cocoa and cornflour mixture and bring to the boil, stirring all the time. Reduce the heat and simmer for 1 minute, stirring continuously.
3. Allow the sauce to cool, stirring occasionally to prevent a skin forming. Add the rum, a tablespoon at a time, mixing well after each addition.
4. Cut the pineapple into chunks. Halve the strawberries and cut the kiwi fruit into chunks. Cover the fruit with clingfilm and put to one side until ready to serve.
5. Stir the chocolate rum sauce well, spoon into four individual ramekins or dishes and arrange the pineapple, strawberries and kiwi fruit around each dish of sauce. Halve the apricots and cut each half into three or four pieces. Place with the prepared fruit and serve each portion with a fork or stick so the fruit can be dipped in the sauce before eating.

STRAWBERRY BRULÉE

Serves 2

215 Calories per serving

To ensure success, take care not to overcook the eggs and grill the completed recipe very quickly, so that the sugar is caramelised without the custard being recooked.

7½oz (225g) strawberries, halved

½ medium orange

For the custard:

¼ pint (150ml) skimmed milk

2 eggs, beaten

1 tablespoon caster sugar

For the topping:

4 teaspoons caster sugar

Exchanges per serving: Fruit 1
Milk ¼
Protein 1
70 Optional
Calories

1. Divide the strawberries between two ramekins. Finely grate the zest from the orange and reserve to flavour the custard. Squeeze the juice and pour over the strawberries.
2. Heat the milk until steaming.
3. Beat the eggs and 1 tablespoon of caster sugar together; gradually mix in the steaming milk. Pour into the top of a double saucepan or a bowl standing over a pan of simmering water.
4. Stir continuously until the custard thickens. This will take some time, especially if using a china or glass bowl. As soon as the custard thickens, remove from the heat and strain, then stir in the grated orange zest. Leave to cool.
5. Spoon the cold custard over the strawberries and sprinkle the top evenly with the remaining caster sugar.
6. Place under a preheated grill and cook until golden and bubbling. Chill before serving.

PIPPA'S PINEAPPLE

Serves 3
115 Calories per serving

This attractive dessert can be made in a matter of minutes. I have suggested using the same proportions of quark-style and curd cheeses, but use all curd cheese if you prefer. The quark gives it a slightly sharper flavour.

½ small pineapple

½ medium papaya

1 kiwi fruit

2oz (60g) quark cheese

2oz (60g) curd cheese

2½ teaspoons set honey

finely grated zest of ¼ a lemon

Exchanges per serving: Fruit 1
Protein ½
40 Optional
Calories

1. Use a grapefruit knife to scoop out the pineapple flesh and leave the skin whole – this makes an ideal serving dish. Chop the pineapple.
2. Remove the round black seeds from the papaya, peel the skin and chop the flesh.
3. Peel the kiwi fruit and cut about four whole slices for decoration. Either chop the remaining fruit or cut into half slices.
4. Mix the cheeses, honey and lemon zest together. Stir in most of the pineapple and papaya, reserving a few pieces for decoration. Add the chopped or half slices of kiwi fruit.
5. Spoon the cheese and fruit mixture back into the pineapple skin and decorate with the reserved fruit.

CHERRY CHOUX PUFFS

Serves 4

315 Calories per serving

These delicious choux puffs are hardly a dessert you'd think you could eat while losing weight – yet you can eat and enjoy them as part of an extra special meal.

For the puffs:

6 tablespoons water

8 teaspoons margarine

2oz (60g) strong bread flour or plain flour

2 eggs, lightly beaten

For the filling:

6oz (180g) curd cheese

2oz (60g) cherries, stoned and chopped

4 tablespoons low-fat natural yogurt

1½ teaspoons caster sugar

For the sauce:

8oz (240g) cherries, stoned

juice of 1 medium orange

4 teaspoons sugar

strip of lemon zest

1½ teaspoons arrowroot

½–1 teaspoon lemon juice

To serve:

½ teaspoon icing sugar

2oz (60g) cherries to decorate

Exchanges per serving: Bread ½
Fat 2
Fruit 1
Protein 1¼
40 Optional
Calories

1. Line a baking sheet with non-stick baking parchment.
2. To make the choux pastry puffs, gently heat the water and margarine in a saucepan until the margarine has melted; increase the heat and bring to a rolling boil. Tip in all the flour and beat well over a low heat for 1 minute. By this time the mixture will be in a ball. Allow to cool a little.
3. Gradually add the eggs, two teaspoons at a time, beating well after each addition. Either spoon or pipe the pastry onto the prepared baking sheet to form 20 small balls.
4. Preheat the oven at Gas Mark 6, 200°C, 400°F. Immediately the puff balls are in the oven, increase the temperature to Gas Mark 7, 210°C, 425°F. Bake for 15 minutes until well risen and golden brown. Make a slit in each puff with a sharp knife to allow the steam to escape. Return to the oven for a further 5 minutes. Cool on a wire rack.
5. To prepare the filling, mix together the curd cheese, cherries, yogurt and sugar. Don't fill the puffs until a short while before serving.
6. To make the sauce, place the cherries, orange juice, sugar and lemon zest in a saucepan. Simmer for about 10 minutes until the cherries are cooked. Remove the lemon zest and transfer to a blender or food processor and process until smooth.
7. Blend a little of the sauce with the arrowroot, gradually add all the sauce and bring to the boil over a moderate heat, stirring all the time. Boil for 1 minute, add lemon juice to taste and leave to cool.
8. Fill the cold choux puffs with a little of the curd cheese filling. Pile five puffs onto each serving plate, dust with a little icing sugar and decorate with the reserved cherries. Spoon a little of the cherry sauce over and serve the remainder separately.

Top: Cherry Choux Puffs *Centre:* Beef Marsala *(p 208)* *Bottom:* Star Starter *(p 19*

BLACKCURRANT SORBET

Serves 6

140 Calories per serving

This sorbet is ideal served with fresh fruit and garnished with mint or tiny blackcurrant leaves, or served with the Grapefruit and Orange Sherbet (page 220).

For the purée:

10oz (300g) blackcurrants

4 tablespoons water

For the syrup:

6fl oz (180ml) water

8 tablespoons sugar

2 egg whites

pinch of cream of tartar

Exchanges per serving: 140 Optional Calories

1. Remove the stalks from all the blackcurrants and place in a saucepan with 4 tablespoons of water. Cover and simmer over a low to moderate heat for 5–8 minutes or until cooked.
2. Transfer the blackcurrants and their juice to a blender and process until smooth. Sieve, pressing the blackcurrant pulp against the sieve to remove as much juice as possible.
3. To make the syrup, heat the water and sugar gently until the sugar has dissolved, then boil rapidly for 2 minutes. Allow to cool, then stir into the sieved blackcurrant purée.
4. Freeze the blackcurrant mixture for about 3 hours, stirring from time to time until a slushy consistency is obtained.
5. Whisk the egg whites and cream of tartar until peaking. Gently fold through the half-frozen blackcurrant mixture with a metal spoon.
6. Return to the freezer for several hours or overnight.

CRÊPES SUZETTE

Serves 4

270 Calories per serving

A flambéed dish always creates a spectacular end to a dinner party, and this delicious low-calorie version of the traditional recipe is no exception.

For the pancakes:

4oz (120g) plain flour

pinch of salt

1 egg

½ pint (300ml) skimmed milk

1 tablespoon margarine or vegetable oil

For the sauce:

2 medium oranges, zest and juice

finely grated zest of ½ a lemon

4 tablespoons sugar

3 tablespoons brandy

Exchanges per serving: Bread 1
Fat ¾
Fruit ½
Milk ¼
Protein ¼
85 Optional Calories

---

1. To make the pancakes, sieve the flour and salt into a bowl, make a well in the centre, add the egg and gradually beat or whisk in the milk.
2. Prove a 7-inch (18-cm) frying pan by generously sprinkling salt over the base, heating gently, tipping out the salt and then wiping the pan thoroughly with kitchen paper. This will prevent the pancakes sticking.
3. Heat a little margarine or oil in the pan and wipe again with kitchen paper.
4. Heat a little margarine in the frying pan, pour in some batter while turning the pan so it thinly coats the base. Cook over a moderate heat until the underside is golden brown, toss or turn over and cook the other side.
5. Transfer the cooked pancake to a plate, cover and keep warm in a low oven while repeating the procedure to make 15 or 16 pancakes.
6. Finely grate the zest from the oranges. Place the orange zest and juice, lemon zest and sugar in a large frying pan, heat gently until the sugar dissolves, increase the heat and boil for 1 minute. Remove from the heat.
7. Dip each side of each pancake in the sauce, fold into quarters and lay on a plate. Repeat with every pancake. Place all the pancakes in the sauce and heat gently. Add the brandy and set alight. Allow the flames to die down, then serve immediately.

APRICOT CHEESECAKE

Serves 6

260 Calories per serving

Use a deep, loose-bottomed flan tin for this recipe or the filling will spill over the edge. This recipe gives really generous portions!

For the base:

6 large digestive biscuits

3 tablespoons margarine

For the topping:

7 medium apricots

1 tablespoon lemon juice

5oz (150g) curd cheese

5 tablespoons caster sugar

few drops of almond essence

2 tablespoons hot water

1 sachet gelatine

2 egg whites

pinch of cream of tartar

4oz (120g) fromage frais

For the decoration:

1 medium apricot

½ teaspoon lemon juice

2½oz (75g) raspberries

Exchanges per serving: **Bread 1**
Fat 1½
Fruit ¾
Protein ¾
55 Optional
Calories

1. Place the biscuits in a plastic bag and crush with a rolling pin to make fine crumbs. Melt the margarine and stir in the biscuit crumbs. Mix well, then press into a serving flan dish or loose-bottomed 8-inch (20-cm) flan tin.
2. Plunge 7 apricots in boiling water and leave for 1 minute. Drain and place in cold water. Remove the skin from each apricot, halve and discard the stones. Transfer the apricot halves and lemon juice to a blender and process until smooth.
3. Beat together the curd cheese and caster sugar, mix in the apricot purée and stir in the almond essence.
4. Pour the hot water into a cup or small basin, sprinkle in the gelatine and stir well. Stand the cup in a saucepan of simmering water and leave until the gelatine has completely dissolved.
5. Stir the dissolved gelatine into the cheese and apricot purée. Leave until beginning to set.
6. Whisk the egg whites and cream of tartar until peaking. Using a metal tablespoon, fold the fromage frais and then the egg whites evenly into the cheese and apricot mixture. Spoon the mixture onto the biscuit base and chill until completely set.
7. To serve, halve the apricot, remove the stone and cut the fruit into thin wedges. Brush each wedge with lemon juice. If the cheesecake is in a loose-bottomed tin, carefully remove by sliding a spatula or palette knife under the biscuit base and sliding the cheesecake onto a plate. Decorate with the apricot wedges and raspberries.

GRAPEFRUIT AND ORANGE SHERBET

Serves 6

90 Calories per serving

Sorbet or sherbet used to be served before a main-meal roast to clear the palate, but nowadays they are usually served as dessert. This one is particularly refreshing.

2 medium pink grapefruit (or ordinary grapefruit if these are not available)

2 medium oranges

1 lemon

4fl oz (120ml) boiling water

For the syrup:

7 tablespoons sugar

4fl oz (120ml) water

2 egg whites

pinch of cream of tartar

sprigs of mint

Exchanges per serving: Fruit 1
80 Optional
Calories

1. Peel the zest from the grapefruit, oranges and lemon and place in a basin. Pour over the boiling water and leave until cool.
2. Squeeze the juice from all the fruit and place in the refrigerator.
3. Place the sugar in a saucepan, add the cold water and heat gently until the sugar has dissolved. Increase the heat and boil rapidly for 1–2 minutes.
4. Strain the water from the fruit zest and stir into the chilled fruit juice. Add the warm syrup and freeze for about 3 hours, stirring from time to time until a 'slushy' consistency is obtained.
5. Whisk the egg whites and cream of tartar until peaking and fold through the half-frozen fruit mixture. Return to the freezer for several hours or overnight.
6. To serve, scoop into serving glasses and garnish with sprigs of mint.

CARIBBEAN SORBET

Serves 6

95 Calories per serving

I first tasted mango and papaya when I visited Trinidad and Tobago many years ago. I enjoyed them so much I frequently include them in cooking, and this sorbet makes a refreshing end to a meal, either alone or accompanied by other tropical fruit.

1 medium orange

½ lemon

6 tablespoons caster sugar

7fl oz (210ml) water

1 medium ripe mango

1 medium ripe papaya

2 egg whites

pinch of cream of tartar

Exchanges per serving: 95 Optional Calories

1. Remove the zest from the orange and lemon half using a potato peeler and place it in a saucepan with the caster sugar and water. Heat gently until the sugar has dissolved, then boil gently for 1–2 minutes. Leave to cool.
2. Cut the mango either side of the stone, scoop out all the flesh and place in a blender or food processor. Remove all the flesh from round the stone and add to the blender.
3. Halve the papaya, discard the round black seeds and scoop out all the flesh into the blender or food processor.
4. Squeeze the juice from the orange and lemon and add to the other fruit. Process until completely smooth.
5. Strain the syrup and stir into the fruit purée. Freeze the purée for 2–3 hours, stirring occasionally, until it has a slushy consistency.
6. Whisk the egg whites and cream of tartar until peaking and fold into the half-frozen purée. Return to the freezer and leave for several hours or overnight before serving.

INDEX

Top: Blackcurrant Sorbet *(p 216)*
Bottom: Grapefruit and Orange Sherbet